Hooked
IN THE HEART

Appreciating the Artistry of God in Everyday Life

SCOTT C. GRANT

Scripture taken from The Holy Bible, New International
Version, © 1973, 1978, 1984 by International Bible Society.

Cover design by André Hawkins

ISBN: 0985490012
ISBN-13: 9780985490010

To Karen
In the quietness of her soul, I have found rest

Contents

Preface

DIVINE SUBTLETY

When I first began wondering whether God existed, I thought it would be easy to believe in him if he just showed up. I also thought it would be easy to follow him if he just told me what to do. I have since come to understand that God takes a more subtle approach.

He wants something more than simple belief and unthinking obedience. He wants our hearts. Therefore, he doesn't foist himself on us like a demanding tyrant. Instead, he enchants us like a skillful artist.

Michelangelo's sculpture of David is a masterpiece not least because of the artist's attention to detail. I had seen photographs of it, but until I saw it in person, I hadn't noticed the look on David's face. His furrowed brow and distant eyes portray a man with much on his mind. When I noticed David's face, I was intrigued to the point of being captivated. The skillful subtlety of Michelangelo, which I had failed to recognize in photographs, took my breath away when I saw his masterpiece in person.

Recognizing the artistry of God requires us to cultivate attentiveness to the subtlety of his ways. He rewards those who cultivate such attentiveness not simply by convincing them of his existence and telling them what to do but by taking their breaths away.

We cultivate attentiveness to God not only by making time for him but also by being open to interruptions, roadblocks, and patterns. If I'm oblivious to the presence of God, an interruption prods me to take notice. If I'm intent on doing things my way, a roadblock redirects me to consider God's way. If the chapters of my life seem disconnected from the story of my life, an unexpected pattern opens my eyes to see God's handiwork.

We also cultivate attentiveness to God by being sensitive to the Scriptures and to the ways in which our stories converge with the biblical story. When I study the Scriptures, I attempt to apply them to life. When I'm away from the Scriptures (which is, of course, most of the time), I attempt to take life and bring it to the Scriptures. When I see my story reflected in the biblical story, perhaps the divine artist is revealing himself.

I make my home in the Silicon Valley, which doesn't stop for God. It hasn't been easy, with everything moving so fast and most people chasing after something, but I've tried to stop. I want to keep up with everything and everyone, but I'd rather keep up with God.

In this collection of vignettes, I've written of my experience with the artistry of God in everyday life. Some of the psalmists conclude their prayers by vowing to share their stories with their countrymen. I share my stories, more or less chronologically, with some adjustment for thematic connections, in hope of helping others sense the artistry of God in their lives.

In the twenty years that these stories span, I suffered a broken engagement and other relational disappointments before welcoming first a wife and then two daughters into my life. I also found a new vocation—that of a pastor. This collection in particular chronicles the relational and vocational aspects of my journey.

The scenes in these stories include churches and trout streams, pulpits and golf courses, highways and parking lots, movie theaters and coffee houses, an abbey and a prison, a gymnasium and an orphanage, a four-star hotel and a Third World hut, a field of thousands and a table for two. The stories are populated by friends and antagonists, acquaintances and strangers, adults and children. I've usually been awake when I've sensed God's artistry, but at least once I was asleep. God can use any place, any person, and any time to make himself known to us.

God doesn't beat us over the head with his presence. He intrigues us, surprises us, and finally captivates us. He reveals himself in ways that delight our hearts. God hooks us. He gets our attention and pulls us away from our concerns to show us his perspective and take our breaths away. He hooks us with his artistry—hooks us right in the heart.

Chapter 1

COMING HOME TO SOMEPLACE NEW

THE LONG WAY HOME

In the fall of 1993, I loaded all my earthly possessions into a two-door hatchback and left Idaho, where I had lived for three years, for California, where I had grown up. How long I would stay I did not know. My plans were vague, and I was apprehensive. I took the long way home, through the northern reaches of California, to allow for a side trip to Hat Creek, a once-great fishery.

As a youth on the banks of Hat Creek, I fell in love with fly-fishing, casting to large rainbow and brown trout. When I lived in California, I would usually take several trips a year to fish Hat Creek. But as the years went by, the fishing deteriorated. The number of fish dwindled, as did their size. I lamented the change, and my trips became less frequent.

When I took my side trip, I didn't intend to fish Hat Creek. The stream was sort of an old friend, and I just wanted to visit it again and see how it was doing. I pulled into my old parking spot and hiked upstream along my favorite stretch. I spotted a solitary fisherman and asked him how he was doing.

"Nothing but small ones," he mumbled.

"Years ago, this part of the stream was filled with big ones," I said.

He nodded knowingly and lamented, "Memories are the only reason to fish here anymore."

Hat Creek, the cherished stream of my youth, had changed. The best you could pull out of the stream anymore were a few memories.

What would I find upon my return to the Santa Clara Valley, the home of my youth? I knew that it had changed; it had become the Silicon Valley. Would it, too, be good for a few memories but nothing else?

All things and all people change—some for the good, some for the not-so-good—with maybe a few exceptions. Places change; times change; styles change; methods change. An approach that achieved results yesterday fails today; one that works in one place doesn't work in another. What can you trust in?

The writer of Hebrews says, "Jesus Christ is the same yesterday and today and forever" (Hebrews 13:8). Jesus is always good. And he's Lord. Faith in him guarantees a positive outcome.

It therefore doesn't matter so much whether Hat Creek changes or California changes. It doesn't matter so much if everything I cherish changes for the worse, because Jesus will be with me for the better today and forever, just as he was with me yesterday. If the place changes, Jesus will be with me in that place.

After my exchange with the nostalgic fisherman, I moseyed back to my car and headed for home. Hat Creek, my old friend in the mountains, wasn't doing so well. I hoped for better things back in the Valley.

THE DAY OF SMALL THINGS

When I woke up the day after moving into a studio apartment, I felt claustrophobic. I had always lived with housemates in dwellings with multiple rooms. Now I felt restricted and lonely.

Later that morning, I would be heading out for my first day at a new job. I had worked for eleven years as a journalist. Now I was seeking work as a pastor, but I wasn't turning up anything. So I had called some friends who owned a frame shop and asked if they needed part-time help. They offered me a job framing pictures but could pay me only slightly more than minimum wage. Income wasn't a concern for me then; I simply needed to do something while I looked for full-time work. Still, at age thirty-six, I felt ashamed of this job.

I had just moved into a small apartment, and I was just about to start a small job. I felt . . . small.

I turned in my Bible to Zechariah 4, as my daily reading schedule dictated. When the Israelites began to rebuild their temple, some of the old men wept because it seemed to them that this version wouldn't measure up to the original (Ezra 3:12). Through the prophet Zechariah, God spoke to this concern. He also spoke to my concern. I heard his voice in Zechariah 4:10: "For who has despised the day of small things?"

For me, it was a day of small things—a small apartment, which I had just occupied, and a small job, which I was about to start. And I had despised the day. Now God, it seemed, was telling me to appreciate it. As it turned out, there was much to appreciate.

The apartment was owned by a family of seven who lived next door. We became fast friends, and the children came calling often. They filled my apartment with joy. I learned about marriage and family—and I would be married with children of my own one day.

The frame shop was owned by a couple whose employees were mostly unreliable teenagers. My friends valued my help and my companionship. We talked of life while laboring together. Working with wood reminded me of Jesus, who labored as a carpenter. While framing pictures that would decorate houses for years, I thought, "I'm bringing beauty to people's lives." I learned about friendship, and about humility.

I worked at the frame shop for four months before moving on to my current job as a pastor. I lived in the apartment for eighteen months before moving into a house with three other men.

I learned from the apartment and the frame shop—and from Zechariah: the day of small things is not to be despised.

On the way to work

Jordan, my six-year-old neighbor, was trying to drag a large tub of water into her backyard, but it was too heavy for her. She pushed and pulled, but the tub wouldn't budge.

I was on my way to work when I noticed her, and I was taken by her plight. I considered carrying the tub to the backyard for her. That way, I wouldn't lose much time. But the quick way isn't always the best way.

"Jordan," I said, "I'll help you. Let's do it together."

"Okay," she said.

Jordan grabbed one handle, and I grabbed the other. Together, we hoisted the tub and carried it to the backyard.

I didn't want to watch her suffer, trying to do the impossible. Yet I didn't want to do it for her; that wouldn't have been any fun. I wanted to help her, but I wanted her to know that she had a part to play. More than anything, I wanted Jordan to know that I wanted to be with her. I wanted her to know it was more important for me to be with her than to go to work.

What's important to God? We're important to God. He fashioned us to serve him in his world. Sometimes, the tasks he gives us seem impossible for us to complete.

God asked Moses to bring the Israelites out of Egypt. Moses thought God was asking the impossible. In a sense, Moses was right. He couldn't do it—at least not alone. But God wasn't asking him to do it alone (Exodus 3).

Moses told God, "Who am I, that I should go to Pharaoh and bring the Israelites out of Egypt?"

God told Moses, "I will be with you."

After stopping to help Jordan, I remembered the interchange between God and Moses. What I wanted to do for Jordan, I think, is what God wanted to do for Moses. Moses was incapable of moving the Israelites, just as Jordan was incapable of moving the tub. God could have carried the people to the wilderness by himself, just as I could have carried the tub to the backyard by myself. Instead, God said to Moses, in so many words, "Let's do it together." Moses had a part to play, and God would help him. God was also saying, "I want to be with you."

What's it like to be God? If God has made humans in his image, somewhat like him, the question isn't totally unanswerable. Sometimes, often when we least expect it, when we're, say, on our way to work, we feel what God feels. I wanted for a six-year-old girl what God wants for me—what God wants for all of us. I wanted her to know that I wanted to be with her.

God wants us to know that he wants to be with us.

UNDER THE BRIDGE

Not long after returning to California from Idaho, I was approaching a trout stream I had fished years ago. The waters of Idaho had spoiled me, and I had been depressed about the prospect of wading California waters again.

Nevertheless, as I approached the stream, I was in good spirits. The prior day I had fished a familiar lake, and though the fishing had been mediocre, the weather and scenery had been spectacular, and I had enjoyed a lovely walk around the lake. I had also discovered a new spring creek filled with little rainbows and lined with radiant wildflowers.

California, I reasoned, wasn't so bad after all. The Lord's blessings, even his wild rainbows, aren't limited to Idaho. So as I left my motel room and headed toward the stream, I was thankful and expectant. I wondered what the Lord was going to do next.

My mind drifted back to a time years ago, when I used to fish the stream with my friend Mark, who lived near the stream back then. Mark had since moved away, and I had more or less lost track of him. Together we used to fish a special nighttime insect hatch downstream that usually raised large trout. The only way that part of the stream could be accessed was with a boat, and Mark had one. He also had access to a private stretch of water upstream. I remembered fishing those stretches with my friend and gave thanks for those times.

Wistfully, I thought it would be nice to fish those stretches with Mark again. It was just a thought, not a raging desire. I was content.

The stream sparkled against the backdrop of the snow-capped mountains, and little mayflies began to hatch and flutter. Trout rose for them here and there, but the action was sparse—except under the bridge. Three or four nice fish were rising regularly there. My best opportunity to hook a large trout was under the bridge, but the bridge made casting difficult.

After experimenting with my float tube for a while, I found that I could wrap my legs around a pillar of the bridge and remain stationary. This also allowed me to lean back and cast my fly to the rising trout, unhindered by the bridge. I was able to hook and land two beautiful rainbows. I thanked the Lord for the challenge posed by the bridge and the opportunity to creatively apply a solution. California was looking better.

As I was fishing, a few boats floated by. As one of them approached, I thought I heard my name. Who, way out here, would know me? The boat floated up to me and, unlike the others, stopped. I looked up, and it was Mark. He was with his father, and though he had said my name, he didn't know it was me at the time. Knowing me and my style of fishing, and seeing this character in a float tube under the bridge, he had said to his father, "That looks like something Scott Grant would do." To his surprise, it was Scott Grant. Mark, though he had moved away, had returned with his father for a quick fishing trip.

That night, Mark and I fished the special nighttime hatch downstream. The next morning, we fished the special stretch of water upstream. I didn't even fish that much. I mostly breathed it all in and marveled at God's goodness. After fishing the upstream section, we were invited by the owners of the land to share iced tea on their patio. The sun was warm, the air was clean, and the fellowship was rich. The owners were followers of Jesus, it turned out—and they were delighted to spend an hour with a pastor.

Moses was reluctant to return to Egypt and face the daunting task of liberating the Israelites. Nevertheless, he obeyed God, however fearfully. While Moses was on his way back to Egypt, God sent Aaron, Moses' brother, into the desert to meet him. Moses told Aaron about God's commissioning of him. Aaron had every reason not to believe Moses; after all, it's not every day that God appears to someone in a burning bush and commands him to do the impossible. Yet Aaron believed Moses. Why? Because God sent Aaron to believe Moses and to confirm for him that the path back to Egypt was the right one (Exodus 4:27-31).

Maybe, then, it was more than the current that brought Mark's boat to me. Maybe God sent Mark my way to confirm for me that my path back to California was the right one.

Bait and switch

I grew up in the Valley of Heart's Delight. That's what it was called back then, because it was covered with orchards. I played in its orchards and ate its fruit. But it was the sixties, and the times . . . they were a-changin'. The orchards died out, and the Valley of Heart's Delight became the Silicon Valley.

I left and returned a few times, but in 1990, I was convinced: I was leaving California and would never be back. Three years later I came back, but only to get married and leave again. Or so I thought. The relationship I had returned for needed more time, so a few weeks in the home of my youth turned into a few months.

I was looking for work as a pastor. I wanted to go someplace new, but as I sat in a coffee house one afternoon in my hometown, I heard four different languages being spoken. Turns out that after I left the Valley, the rest of the world arrived. In my absence, it had become someplace new.

So I considered staying. A church was looking to add a pastor to its staff, and I contacted it. We talked, the church offered me a position, and I accepted. The relationship I returned for ended, but the job I wasn't looking for replaced it. God, it seems, pulled the old bait and switch. I returned for one reason, but I stayed for another. I started quoting a line from a song I heard once: "Look how far I had to come / To get back where I started from."[1] I've been quoting it ever since.

I've heard it said that the Silicon Valley has no soul. It focuses on technology, not spirituality. Less than five percent of its residents identify themselves as evangelical believers.

Jesus said, "If anyone is thirsty, let him to me and drink. Whoever believes in me, as the Scripture has said, streams of living water will flow from within him" (John 7:37-38).

As a teenager in the Valley, I tasted the living water. Since returning, I've drunk deeply from the fountain that is Jesus. I've invited many of the Valley's people, some of whom have come from distant lands, to partake as well.

You can find living water here. The orchards are gone, replaced by silicon chips, to be replaced by something else in the future. But the living God still makes his living water available here.

For me, it has become, once again, the Valley of Heart's Delight.

ABBA, FATHER!

I was pacing the streets, trying to come to grips with the ugliness that I was seeing. I was troubled by the sights, for they were observable in a most disturbing place—in me. I saw, more vividly than ever before, my own sinfulness. Perhaps worse than my feelings of sinfulness were my feelings of helplessness. I felt that I couldn't change myself.

I squeezed out a barely audible cry to God: "What do I do?" Immediately I sensed God's response. I heard no words, but I had a strong impression of God's meeting my frantic question in a calm, matter-of-fact manner: "Well, Scott, you have my word." Yes, I had God's word. And though I had been studying and teaching it for years, I knew I needed to turn to the word of God in a fresh way. If I felt helpless to change, and if the Holy Spirit was supposed to change me, I figured I needed to find him. I began reading the New Testament on a painstaking mission to find the Spirit of God.

I found him everywhere, and I found him doing something quite different from what I had expected. I assumed that the Spirit was concerned with the same thing I was: performance. The Spirit was supposed to change my wretchedness and make me a better person, I thought. He was supposed to enable me to live well. He was supposed to give me the power to obey God. But as I crawled through the New Testament, my view of the Holy Spirit began to change, and by the time I reached the fourth chapter of the book of Galatians, I was ready for this: "Because you are sons, God sent the Spirit of his Son into our hearts, the Spirit who calls out, '*Abba,* Father!'"

I was stunned. How many times had I read that verse before, even examining it for subtle nuances? A hundred? Yet I hadn't seen all that was there. I got up from my desk and proclaimed to myself, "That's what the Spirit's about!"

"Abba" is an intimate Aramaic word for "father." The Spirit is about relationship, about showing us the truth of who God is and bringing us closer to him in a Father-son relationship. As we understand at deeper levels who the Father is, and as we become more intimate with him, we are changed. We can't help but be changed. I wanted the change without the relationship, because, as I came to discover as I continued to read, I was afraid of the relationship. So instead, I had chosen performance.

That was nineteen years ago. My fresh look at the New Testament was the foundation for spiritual reformation in my life. Oh, I still try to crank up obedience—the performance ethic in me runs deep. But the Spirit's soft and tender voice is more intelligible. I hear him calling out, and now I cry out with him, "*Abba*, Father!"

THE FOURTH FLOOR

In the wake of a broken relationship, I wanted to take a personal retreat and meet with God. I casually mentioned my interest to a friend, and she mentioned a church in Inverness, north of San Francisco. I didn't know where else to try, so I followed up on her recommendation. I made a phone call and booked a room for a two-day retreat.

In late December 1995, I woke up early and departed for St. Columba Episcopal Church. I drove from my home in the Santa Clara Valley and through San Francisco. I crossed the Golden Gate Bridge, navigated a narrow mountain road to Highway 1, and leisurely worked my way up the coast, taking in the breathtaking vistas. At 11:00 a.m., I arrived at the town of Inverness and followed a sign up a hill to St. Columba.

The building looked more like a haunted house than a church. It had four floors, hidden stairwells, and oddly positioned rooms. The place seemed eerily abandoned. After several minutes of poking around, I found a parishioner, who pointed me in the direction of the retreat rooms on fourth floor.

Still, I took a couple of wrong turns. I found my way to the third floor and ascended the final, dimly lit staircase, my suitcase bumping against the narrow walls.

I read the sign above the first door at the top of the stairs: St. Jean Vianney.

I had arrived.

I opened the door and crept through the entryway. Sunlight streamed through the French windows, and the auburn-hued décor almost glowed. The room was perched, like an eagle's nest, at the apex of the pitched roof, affording a panoramic view of the Tomales Bay to my left and the cypress-covered hills before me and to my right.

I reacted with surprised delight. This room seemed designed with me in mind, right down to the antique writing desk. I spent the next two days there in conversation with my Lord.

God liberated his people from Egypt and led them by his Spirit to the wilderness, where they met with him in the tabernacle, and to the Promised Land, where they met with him in the temple. The journey to the wilderness and on to the Promised Land was fraught with twists and turns, not to mention starts and stops, but God saw to it that his people met with him in the places of his choosing.

Today we have neither tabernacle nor temple, but there remain, I fathom, settings that God designs, or has a hand in designing, that are particularly suited for meeting with him. Although it's true that God is just as present in one place as he is in another, it's also true that he knows what helps each of us meet with him. There remain, then, for each of us, special places—places we might even call holy— that his Spirit leads us to.

For me, the fourth floor at St. Columba is such a place. Since my first retreat, I've met with God there at least once a year, every year. The holy place wasn't easy to find, but I suspect I had some help finding it.

TO LOVE AND BE LOVED

What is it that I really want? I want many things, of course, but what do I want most? Or, do all the things I want really originate from something central? Can all my desires be explained by something at the core?

It was a particularly low moment. I was feeling rejected on the one hand and accused on the other. Movement helps me think and pray, so I went for a long walk. Eventually, I arrived at the question, "What do I want?" I could have asked the question of myself at any other time and pried loose dozens of answers. This day, I considered it for only an instant before these words erupted from within me: "I want to love and be loved!"

That's it, isn't it? I want to love and be loved. That's what I want most; that's the thing at the core.

Why did I answer the question in this way on this day? I was pouring out my heart to God. When you articulate your grief, you access your heart. What's in your heart then surfaces so that you can know what you actually believe. Because I was in pain, I poured out my heart to God and discovered that I want to love and be loved.

I want to love, but my love doesn't seem to be enough; that's why I was in pain. I want to be loved, but I'm never loved enough; that's also why I was in pain. I'm unreliable, and so, it seems, is everyone else. I know what I really want, but what I really want is out of reach. Or is it?

King David encourages me: "But I am a worm and not a man, / scorned by men and despised by the people. / All who see me mock me; / they hurl their insults, shaking their heads"

(Psalm 22:6). Love failed him, but he didn't give up on it. Listen: "Though my father and mother forsake me, / the Lord will receive me" (Psalm 27:10). Literally, David says the Lord will "gather" him. The failure of human love—his love for others, their love for him—drove him to the arms of divine love. In the presence of God, it didn't matter that David didn't love well. God received him nonetheless.

Do you see? It matters if I don't love others well. I mean, it seems to affect their love for me. But it doesn't matter whether I don't love God well. Oh, I guess it matters, but it doesn't change his love for me. He will receive me. When human love breaks me into pieces, God will gather me. I want to be loved, and I am loved—by God.

But I also want to love. I want to love God, yes, but I want to love others as well, or at least better than I do now. How is this possible?

The apostle John encourages me: "This is love: not that we loved God but that he loved us and sent his Son as an atoning sacrifice for our sins. Dear friends, since God so loved us, we also ought to love one another" (1 John 4:10-11). God's love for me has the potential to deepen my love for others. It figures that if my appreciation of God's love for me deepens, my love for others will also deepen. God's love can liberate me to do what I want: to love.

If I'm loved by God, and if I more deeply love others, it stands to reason that I'll also be loved by others. If I believe God loves me, I won't need them to love me as much, and they'll respond not because I need them to love me but because they're free to love me.

If I want to love and be loved, I need to believe God loves me. The failure of human love, though it may drive me into the arms of divine love, also makes me suspicious of love—any love, including God's. How can I believe God loves me?

The Lord Jesus encourages me: "I am the good shepherd. The good shepherd lays down his life for the sheep" (John 10:11). Why would Jesus lay down his life for me and serve as an atoning sacrifice for my sins unless he loved me? This is the love I need: love that is unquestionably selfless and costly. "Greater love has no one than this," Jesus said, "that he lay down his life for his friends" (John 15:13).

To love and be loved—maybe it's not out of reach.

Gym rules

I consider exercise a necessary waste of time. My objective, when I go to the gym, is to complete my workout as quickly as possible. I'd rather play a sport, but a knee injury restricts me. So I trudge on down to the gym two or three times a week.

A list of rules is posted at my gym for people who use the weight machines. I use the machines by proceeding in order, from one to another, until I'm finished with the circuit. I therefore appreciate the rule that prohibits users from cutting in front of those who are following the circuit. This rule, however, is often ignored, much to my chagrin.

Another rule commands users to wipe down the machines after they're finished. This rule does not capture my fancy. In days gone by, I played a little ball. Sweat doesn't bother me. My sweat, your sweat—I'm fine with it. Because I want to complete my workout as quickly as possible, I don't want to take the time to wipe down each machine.

One day, when someone cut in front of me, I sighed with disdain, but in an undetectable way. Moments later, after I had proceeded to another machine without wiping down the previous apparatus, the user who followed me cast a disdainful glance in my direction as he wiped my sweat from the machine he was about to use.

Well, wasn't I the hypocrite?

The Pharisees thought they occupied the moral high ground, but Jesus castigated them for preferring the parts of the law that suited them over its more challenging aspects (Matthew 23:23). Until my hypocrisy was exposed, I deemed myself a law-abiding gym user, morally superior to others who didn't obey the rule that I valued.

I wipe down the machines now.

LUNCHTIME THEOLOGY

I was enjoying my lunch while seated at a table outside a restaurant on a summer afternoon in Palo Alto, not far from where I work. Suddenly, without warning, water came streaming from above and drenched a man who was walking by. Stunned, he removed his glasses and looked around for answers. It rarely rains in Palo Alto in the summer, and no clouds were in the sky. I got up from my table to help him solve the mystery.

We surmised that the water could have come from any of ten windows in the six-story building he was walking near. Someone—without sinister intent, I presumed—must have poured water out of his or her window. But which window? When we looked up, all the windows were closed.

After composing himself, the victim said, "I'm going to do the civilized thing and not throw rocks."

"Even if you threw rocks," I told him, "you wouldn't know which window to aim at."

"Oh," he said, "I have a lot of time."

The thought of breaking ten windows to retaliate against one perpetrator had obviously crossed his mind. If he had proceeded with such a plan, nine innocent people would have been targets of his wrath. The man's dispute was with one person, but because he couldn't identify that person, he was inclined to strike at others in the vicinity. He restrained himself, however, and walked on.

"What causes fights and quarrels among you?" writes the apostle James. "Don't they come from your desires that battle within you? You want something and don't get it" (James 4:1-2).

23

You want something, like an uneventful stroll down the sidewalk, and don't get it, so you get angry.

If I have a dispute, with whom am I angry? When it comes right down to it, my dispute is with God. If he is all-powerful, as the Scriptures claim, whatever happens to me is under his purview. When I don't get what I want, I tend to get angry. My first reaction, though, is not to get angry with God, whom I can't see, but to get angry with the perpetrator, if I can identify one, or even with people in general—people who just happen to be in the vicinity. I'm really angry with God, but since retaliation against him is problematic, I take out my wrath on others. When I throw rocks at others, so to speak, I'm really throwing rocks at God. If others get angry and throw rocks at me, maybe they're really angry with God and my window just happens to be nearby.

It's always better to deal with the one you're angry at than with those on the periphery. It's better to have it out with God. It's better to do what David did when his enemy gained the upper hand:

> How long, O Lord? Will you forget me forever?
> How long will you hide your face from me?
> How long must I wrestle with my thoughts
> And every day have sorrow in my heart?
> How long will my enemy triumph over me? (Psalm 13:1-2)

I didn't go to lunch for a lesson in theology, but that's what I got.

Two vocations

When I picked journalism for a career, I had no idea I'd later become a pastor. I was a journalist; now I'm a pastor. They're two unrelated vocations, right? That's the common assumption when people find out that I used to be a journalist. That was also my assumption when I left the news business for the sheep business. But the more I got into my second vocation, the more it felt like my first.

In my newspaper career, I worked as both a reporter and an editor.

As a pastor, I started teaching the Scriptures. I felt as if I were reporting. The stories were different; they featured the human quest for God instead of the news of the day, but they were still stories. And I'd been telling stories for years.

When I started studying the Scriptures, I felt as if I were editing copy. I saw that the biblical authors were, in a way, reporters. The authors were confusing at times, but no less so than some of the reporters I worked with. And I'd been working with reporters for years.

When I started counseling, I felt as if I were interviewing. As a reporter, I asked sources questions so that I could get to the bottom of the story. As a pastor, in order to offer someone helpful counsel, I needed to get to the bottom of his or her story. I had to ask the right questions. And I'd been asking people questions for years.

King Saul didn't think David, a shepherd boy, could take Goliath. David told him:

Your servant has been keeping his father's sheep. When a lion or a bear came and carried off a sheep from the flock, I went after it, struck it and rescued the sheep from its mouth. When it turned on me, I seized it by its hair, struck it and killed it. Your servant has killed both the lion and the bear; this uncircumcised Philistine will be like one of them, because he has defied the armies of the living God. The Lord who delivered me from the paw of the lion and the bear will deliver me from the hand of this Philistine. (1 Samuel 16:34-37)

David defeated Goliath. And why not? He'd been killing giants for years. More or less, he knew how to do it. He didn't know he'd fight Goliath one day, but God knew.

As a pastor, I think like a journalist. It's the kind of pastor God made me and trained me to be. I'm always asking, "What's the story?" More or less, I know how to do it. I didn't know I'd be a pastor one day, but I guess God knew.

I thought I chose journalism. But maybe God, knowing his plans for me, chose it for me.

A LITTLE FAILURE

When I decided to start a ministry for young adults, I asked twelve people to help me and hoped that a handful would say yes. No more than four or five were necessary to get the ball rolling, I figured. To my surprise, eleven said yes, and one of them brought his girlfriend. I asked twelve, and twelve responded. Jesus began with twelve, so I hoped we were off to a good start.

I began meeting weekly with the new team. We didn't talk much about vision; we didn't even develop a vision statement. Mostly, we shared meals, talked, and prayed. After only four team meetings, we launched the Young Adults Fellowship.

Six months later, the only one who declined my invitation to join the team said he was ready to commit. Within a year, the Young Adults Fellowship grew from twelve to about one hundred.

The first ministry I started, on the other hand, wasn't so easy. I spent six months getting to know the church and another six months meeting with a team and crafting a vision. I brooded over the whole process. When we finally launched the ministry, it wasn't what I envisioned, and I wondered, "What was all that preparation for?"

Eventually, the first ministry died. The Young Adults Fellowship, through its various incarnations, thrived. I think my different approach to the second ministry helped. I had to fail with the first approach, though, to learn a different approach. Mostly, I learned to be less stressed and more relaxed.

I'm still learning, of course. I'm not sure I'll ever be able to completely shake the preposterous belief that I can make life predictable. I know that I can do everything right and be struck down by any one of a thousand maladies. When I was in my twenties, I was in two traffic accidents that easily could have killed me, yet I walked away from both of them. I was at fault in neither of them. Since then, I've been in more traffic accidents, none of which has been my fault. I'm a good driver. But good drivers die on the streets every day. This I know, yet my stubborn belief that my life is in my hands will not die.

Only one thing has helped me relax, really: failure. What I dislike most about failure is that it makes me *feel* like a failure. It makes me feel inadequate. In other words, it makes me feel what I need to feel. The anguish of failure motivates me to release my predictable version of reality and embrace the sovereignty of God.

Moses wanted to deliver his people, the Hebrews, from their Egyptian oppressors. Hoping to inspire an uprising, he struck down an Egyptian who was beating a Hebrew. Before doing so, however, he looked around to see if anyone was watching. Afterward, to cover his tracks, he hid the body in the sand. He was meticulous, but he failed. He looked all around, but not to heaven. The Hebrews wouldn't follow him and the Egyptian king tried to kill him, so he fled to the wilderness. Moses had gone out to deliver his people, but only when he sat down by a well in the wilderness, without trying to do much of anything, did he begin to embrace the sovereignty of God.

Despite Moses' failure—or maybe, in part, because of it—God told him to return to Egypt and deliver the Hebrews. Moses was reluctant but obedient. The anguish of failure taught him to go out with less trust in himself and more trust in God.

The first time, he struck down one Egyptian and hid the body. The second time, God struck down every Egyptian first-born. There was no need to hide the bodies; the land was littered with them (Exodus 2:11-22, 12:12; Acts 7:20-29).

If you want to trust God, it's probably going to take a little failure. Maybe a lot of failure.

WHAT'S IT ALL ABOUT?

I was reminiscing with a longtime friend about when we were in our twenties. In the midst of our conversation, I found myself asking him, "What was that all about, anyway?" We looked at each other, shook our heads, and smiled. Neither of us had a ready answer, only more questions.

What did those years mean? What were we trying to accomplish? Why, at times, did we think and act so foolishly?

After reflecting on that conversation, I came up with an answer for my own question. What was it all about? It was about trying to find a satisfying answer to the question, "Who am I?" Why else would that season in our lives be characterized by such desperate hope? We were hopeful that life would be good, but we had our doubts, so we desperately tried to make it good. We tried to convince ourselves that our efforts were succeeding spectacularly, but our inner lives wouldn't go along with the charade. Consequently, we were always restless, often insecure, and seldom content. We were always suppressing the unspoken question, "Who am I?" All our desperate efforts to make life good were desperate efforts to find out who we were.

I am more than two decades removed from that season now. The question, "Who am I?" has faded. It is still there, but it no longer haunts me—I think because it is being answered by another question: "Who is God?"

Moses asked God, "Who am I, that I should go to Pharaoh and bring the Israelites out of Egypt?" God never answered him. Instead, he said, "I will be with you." The important question isn't, "Who am I?" but, "Who is God?" (Exodus 3:11-12).

As I am finding out who God is, in his power and goodness, I find myself wanting to know him more. Who am I? I'm a child of God, created by him and purchased by Jesus Christ to know him and honor him. I can only answer the question about my identity this way because I'm asking a question about God's identity.

Maybe, also, I can help a few others with their questions by telling them about the one who told Moses, "I am who I am" (Exodus 3:14).

Chapter 2

TRAVELS WITH JESUS

Bumped

I'm usually somewhat shy about introducing myself. This time, buoyed by the enthusiasm of leaving for Brazil, I assumed my seat on the plane, extended my hand to the woman next to me, and said, "Hi, I'm Scott." She reached out her hand and told me her name.

"Where are you from?" I asked.

"Brazil," she said.

That's interesting, I thought. The plane that my three traveling companions and I had just boarded in San Francisco would take us to Los Angeles, where we planned to catch another flight to São Paulo, Brazil. We expected to spend two weeks in São José dos Campos, Brazil, teaching the Scriptures to a church there. The woman explained that she had just finished taking English classes in Berkeley and that she was now returning home—coincidentally on the same two flights.

Her name was Raquel (in Portuguese, it's pronounced Haquel), a twenty-two-year-old Brazilian of Japanese descent. We struck up a conversation, and I introduced her to my companions. One of us asked if she had visited Disneyland while she was in the United States. She said she hadn't been able to.

As we arrived in Los Angeles on Sunday afternoon, we asked Raquel if she'd like to sit with us on the next flight, which was leaving in just a few hours. The five of us together made our way to the international terminal and waited in line at the counter. Just as it was our turn to check our luggage and receive our boarding passes, the airline's computers went down.

We all went to lunch except for Steve, who remained at the counter. When we returned after lunch, a big commotion was taking place at the counter. The airline had overbooked our flight, the five of us had been bumped, and the next flight to São Paulo wasn't for another three days. The airline would put us up in a Los Angeles hotel, but there was no way we were getting on that plane.

After the shock wore off, I began thinking that perhaps God had led us to Raquel. We were four people preparing to minister to an entire church. Would God postpone our plans so that the four of us could minister to one, or so that one could minister to the four of us?

The apostle Paul and his companions came to the border of Mysia and planned to head east, to Bithynia, but the Holy Spirit somehow prevented them. During the night, Paul had a vision that convinced him and his companions that God was calling them to head west and preach the gospel in Macedonia. What was wrong with Bithynia? Maybe nothing. The vision didn't say. But God sent them to Macedonia (Acts 16:6-10).

What was wrong with the timing of our plans to go to Brazil? Maybe nothing. God didn't say. But he wouldn't let us get on the plane.

We asked Raquel, "How would you like to go to Disneyland?" Normally reserved, Raquel beamed. Monday, we piled into our rental car and went to Disneyland. That night she told us that she would add to her normal prayer an offer of thanks to God for meeting us. Tuesday, we went to the beach. All the while, we shared our lives with each other. We learned about Raquel, and she learned about us.

Wednesday, we boarded the plane to São Paulo. We arrived in Brazil on Thursday morning—three days later than we had planned but, perhaps, right on schedule. We met Raquel's parents at the airport and bade her farewell, not knowing whether we would meet again but knowing that all five of us were richer because our flight had been overbooked.

STEP BY STEP

As I was leaving a prison I had toured in São José dos Campos, Brazil, I heard music coming from inside the walls. It was the refrain of a familiar song: "And step by step you'll lead me / And I will follow you all of my days."[2] As I was walking away, step by step, somehow I knew that the song was for me.

About a week earlier, after arriving in São José, I had stumbled upon my host family's compact disc player and noticed an album by Michael W. Smith, an American artist. I played it. The words of one song ministered to me: "Just leave it to me / I'll lead you home."[3] Later, after touring the prison, I knew this song and these words were also for me. I went on to play it a half dozen times during our stay, and it resonated with me each time.

I traveled to a different continent, and these two songs from home were waiting for me. In a land of strange tongues, these songs came to me in my tongue. In a land where I couldn't understand two words, I understood two songs. In a land where no two sentences seemed related, two melodies harmonized. And in a land where I should have understood nothing, I understood that God was speaking to me—softly, clearly: "Just leave it to me / I'll lead you home." And I answered: "Step by step you'll lead me / And I will follow you all of my days."

I went to Brazil with two companions in the summer of 1996 to teach the Scriptures to a church in São José. Something strange happened after we arrived: I relaxed. I realized, based on the ease with which I experienced Brazil, that back home, in my land, my perfectionism was getting the better of me. Because

I wanted everything to be perfect, I was never satisfied and I could never relax. And I guess I wasn't all that easy to be around.

One of my traveling companions told me, "I had no idea you were this much fun." If a friend had to leave the continent to find out that I was fun, I knew that something was wrong.

"Come to me," Jesus said, "all you who are weary and burdened, and I will give you rest. Take my yoke upon you and learn from me, for I am gentle and humble in heart, and you will find rest for your souls. For my yoke is easy and my burden is light" (Matthew 11:28-30).

When I realized in Brazil that I was weary and burdened, I cried out to God, "How do I get out of this mess?"

I don't think I expected an answer, but that afternoon, an answer came, step by step, outside the prison walls. Ah, yes. How do I get out of this mess, this prison? Step by step you'll lead me, and I will follow you all of my days. Yes, Lord, you'll lead, and I'll follow. I'm leaving the prison, even now, and you're leading me. And I'm hearing you: "Just leave it to me; I'll lead you home."

Perfectionism is still with me, but not like before. The Lord has led me. And I guess I have followed.

LOVE SO BEAUTIFUL

I didn't expect to be surprised the second time I visited Brazil. The first time, God had met me in a powerful way and jolted me. Lightning never strikes twice, especially if you're watching for it. How can God surprise me if I'm hoping he'll surprise me? He surprised me anyway.

During my first missions trip to Brazil, I had been shocked by how relaxed I was able to be. The Lord had showed me, by virtue of the ease with which I experienced Brazil, that I was leading a life of unrest back home, creating and carrying unnecessary burdens. For two weeks, I had taught the Scriptures to the Free Methodist Church in São José dos Campos, feeling nary an ounce of pressure.

So when I returned to the church in Brazil the next year with three companions from my church in California, I expected to delight in the reunion with friends and to perhaps choke back a few tears. But I didn't expect to choke back tears the whole night. I frequently experience momentary bursts of joy or sadness that affect me deeply but pass quickly, like a door opening and closing. This time the door stayed open.

I was seated in the church as Clovis, one of its members, led us in song. If I sang, the tears would come. If I even looked at Clovis or anyone else in the church, the tears would come. So I didn't sing, and I didn't look. After Clovis asked my companions and me to lead the church in a song I had taught them the previous year, I lifted my head briefly and caught a glimpse of the beaming face of Esther, a woman who had been particularly encouraged by our teaching. I knew I could look up no more. So I stared at the floor and mumbled the words to "Lord, I Lift Your Name on High."

What was happening? As I saw these people, I remembered the previous year—how God met me through them. The first night back, I saw their love for each other and their love for me, both of which had liberated me the previous year. I thought, once again, of my life back home and, sadly, of my obsession with effectiveness.

I want to accomplish. I want to succeed. I want to be effective. More than that, I want to be effective so that I can feel good about myself. I'm seeking not so much effectiveness as I am validation. If I'm effective, according to my thinking, I'm valid. I'm somebody. I'm significant.

Validity, though, comes from God. I'm somebody and I'm significant because I've been created in the image of God and redeemed by the blood of his Son. To seek validation outside of God's love for me is to run from my Creator and Redeemer (Genesis 1:26-27, Colossians 1:13-14).

What's more, if effectiveness is my aim, that means I'm trying to measure it. Anytime I make something a goal, I can't help but constantly assess my progress. How do I measure effectiveness? Am I effective if I preach a good sermon? Answer difficult questions? Attract lots of attention?

I saw people who were attracting very little attention, yet they were effective. I was feeling their effect. I was feeling their love. That first night back, I saw love. I saw love so beautiful that it caused me to shudder. I saw love that showed me the vanity of my quest for validation, the hypocrisy of my obsession with effectiveness, and the tragedy of my distance from God. Once again, he surprised me.

THE GOOD HURT

Blaise Pascal is often quoted as speaking of a "God-shaped vacuum" in the human heart. The implication of the metaphor is that only God can fill a certain empty space in our hearts. Yes, I have felt emptiness, but what I feel more often and more acutely is some kind of cross between pain and desire: I want something more than what I have to the extent that it hurts me. David James Duncan, in his novel *The River Why*, gave me a metaphor for what I feel.

Near the end of the story, Gus Orviston hooks a huge salmon on light fishing line. He wants to play the fish, not land it. Play it he does, following the salmon up the river for seven miles. Along the way, Gus develops an affinity for the creature. At the end of his quest, he gets in the water and comes face to face with the fish. He cradles the salmon in his hand and gently releases it. By this time, it's the middle of the night, and Gus begins a seven-mile hike back to his cabin. Gus narrates:

> The road was white with frost: it shone like a strip of moon surface in the early light, running from east to west like the horizontal bar of a cross. The entire valley hovered, still, before me. Somewhere a raven called . . .

> And then I felt it—a sharp pain in the heart, like a hook being set. I whirled around: sunlight struck me full in the face. My eyes closed.

> And then I saw it—the vertical bar—a line so subtle it must be made of nothing nameable. And it ran from my

heart of earth and blood through my head, to the sky; ran like a beam of watery light; ran from the changing, flowing forms of world to a realm that light alone could enter. But my pain grew sharper: mad with joy, I sank to my knees on the white road, and I felt the hand, resting like sunlight on my head. And I knew that the line of light led not to a realm but to a Being, and that the light and the hook were his, and that they were made of love alone. My heart was pierced. I began to weep. I felt the Ancient One drawing me toward him, coaxing me out of this autumn landscape, beckoning me on toward undying joy.

The hand was lifted. The nameless presence faded, and the light around me blended with the sunlight I knew. But in my heart the wound stayed, and the good hurt. I rose from the road, brushed off my knees, wiped my eyes and drew breath. Then I walked—though I knew that from this point on the road, and from this point in my soul, there was no escape, nowhere to go.[4]

Gus' vision relates to what he's just experienced. Only this time, he's the salmon and God has hooked him. In this scene, the Ancient One paints a cross with the horizontal bar of mist and the vertical line of light.

I resonate with Gus. The Ancient One has hooked me with his love. He's drawn me toward him, coaxing me out of whatever landscape I've traversed, beckoning me on toward undying joy. I've felt the hook. I've seen where the line leads. I've seen the cross of his Son. I have felt the hand of the Ancient One.

God has hooked me, just as he hooked Gus. He also hooked the apostle Paul:

> Not that I have already obtained all this, or have already been made perfect, but I press on to take hold of that for which Christ has taken hold of me. Brothers, I do not consider myself yet to have taken hold of it. But one thing I do: Forgetting what is behind and straining toward what is ahead, I press on toward the goal to win the prize for which God has called me heavenward in Christ Jesus. (Philippians 3:12-14)

Christ took hold of Paul that Paul might take hold of him. Having tasted Christ, Paul wants more of Christ, so he presses on. The prize is knowing Christ fully at the end of the race. Paul will not rest until he rests in the eternal presence of Christ.

On the one hand, I can expect to be dissatisfied so that I will always want something more. On the other hand, Christ has taken hold of me that I might seek that "something more" in him. The cross between pain and desire that I feel? I'm supposed to feel it. I'm supposed to feel it that I might press on to know Christ fully. I'm not supposed to be satisfied—at least not completely. Therefore, paradoxically, I can be satisfied with dissatisfaction. Christ must be too great to fully appreciate in one lifetime.

A hook in the heart: that's my metaphor.

Just off the road, just over the rise

I crossed the Golden Gate and headed toward the coast, toward Point Reyes, for a two-day personal retreat. I was looking forward to two days of prayer, reading, and writing at a quaint retreat house in the hills above Tomales Bay. Inasmuch as I had been there before, I looked forward to its beauty with anticipation.

It was a Friday morning, and few cars were on the road. My pace was slow. Just as another car approached from the rear, I noticed a sign that read "Turnout—one-quarter mile." I made plans to turn off and let the car pass. Immediately, I noticed another sign that read "Muir Beach overlook." I assumed this was the turnout that the previous sign flagged, even though it was off to the left. I followed the sign to the left and let the car pass. I then realized that this "turnout" was not a turnout at all. As long as I was there, I decided to drive up the hill to see the Muir Beach overlook.

The detour led to one of the most spectacular views I have ever seen of the Pacific Coast, with a catwalk to a precipice that afforded a vantage point from which I could take in all the beauty of the magnificent setting. The wind was cold, so I didn't stay long—just long enough to gaze north, south, east, west, and up. I raised my hands to praise the Creator of such beauty, the Leader who guided me to this setting.

Isn't God like that? My destination is Tomales Bay. There I will see something beautiful. There I will seek the Lord. But on the way, he finds me. On the way, he wants to show me something beautiful—just off the road, just over the rise. I never would

45

have seen it if a hurried driver hadn't caught up with me at just the right time, if signs hadn't been positioned in just the right places, if I hadn't "mistakenly" pulled off to the left instead of the right.

Isn't life like that? We go about our business, and the Lord interrupts our plans with something better. And when he interrupts with something better, he shows us, most importantly, that he is better—better than our plans, and better than we thought he was. I am learning to keep my eyes peeled for these divine detours, because in them, God shows me himself, and he is the most beautiful sight of all.

A father asked Jesus to come and heal his gravely ill daughter. Jesus went with him but stopped on the way to help an ill woman. Before finishing with the woman, he learned that the girl had died. Jesus told the father, "Don't be afraid; just believe." He resumed his journey to the father's house, where he raised the girl from the dead. The detour resulted in two healings instead of one and turned the first healing into a resurrection. It also pushed the father's faith to the edge and in the end enlarged it (Mark 5:21-43).

After a few minutes on the precipice of the Muir Beach overlook, I returned to my car and resumed my journey. A few hundred feet up the road, I noticed the advertised turnout off to the right. A glance in my rear-view mirror revealed an empty road behind me. There was no need to turn off, so I kept driving. I had already taken the turnout intended for me.

Two guys named John

As John read his story, we were glued to every word. We couldn't hear every word, because John is not an expert at either reading or speaking. He has a disability that inhibits him, both physically and mentally, but he is an expert in things of the heart.

He called his story "My Life on Video." It's the story of how one night, Jesus awakened John and showed him some highlights from his life as if on video. The video showed him as a child wanting to be in a normal class with all the other kids instead of in a special-education class. It showed him as a teenager longing for a girlfriend but being denied. It showed him as an adult agonizing over the loss of a job as a janitor. Nevertheless, John accepted each disappointment.

In the end, Jesus fast-forwards the video to the present and tells John, then forty-four years old, "I showed you this video to show I've been taking care of you. And you can trust in me that I will continue to take care of you. Yes, you are different from your brothers and sisters, but the reason that I made you this way is to glorify God, and also, you will be close to me. And remember that I will always be with you."

About a hundred of us were in attendance at the end of the weekend retreat when John read his story. One of those in the audience was another man named John. John Stothers is one of the most talented people I know. He is an extraordinary musician, singer, songwriter, and worship leader. As John Schreiner read his story, John Stothers sat in the front row. He leaned forward, with his head buried in his hands and his eyes closed. He never moved. He absorbed every word.

I sat off to the side, and I found myself looking back and forth, between the two Johns: the listener and the speaker, the able and the disabled. The one with the obscure gifts was blessing the one with the obvious gifts.

As the weekend came to an end, we each went our separate ways. I thanked John Stothers for leading music at the retreat. He shook his head, obviously moved in some way by what he had experienced, and said softly, his voice cracking, "It's amazing that God can use me." Amazing? That God could use him? Isn't he the kind of person that God uses, he with all the gifts?

Well, yes, he is, but I realized once again that gifts have nothing to do with it and that humility has everything to do with it. Yes, God used him. But God also used the other John.

The apostle Peter quotes Proverbs 3:4, "God opposes the proud but gives grace to the humble." Then he writes, "Humble yourselves, therefore, under God's mighty hand, that he may lift you up in due time" (1 Peter 5:5-6).

God, it seemed to me, lifted up two humble men—two guys named John. In the end, I surmised, they had a lot more in common than their name.

THE DREADED DAY

Early on in my days as a pastor, when I decided to teach the book of Hebrews, I knew that one day I would open the door to my study, sit down at my desk, and see Hebrews 6:4-8 staring back at me. I had read those verses dozens of times without arriving at a satisfying interpretation.

The possible interpretation that I dreaded, the one that many scholars have adopted, is that it is possible for one to be once legitimately saved and then unsaved. I knew all the other passages, the ones that had convinced me that it is not possible for God to abandon one who belongs to him. Yet, Hebrews 6 is no less a part of his word.

I not only believe in the eternal security of the believer in Christ, I also believe in teaching the word of God expositionally—word by word, verse by verse, book by book. Usually, I pick a book in the Bible, start at the beginning, and finish at the end, without skipping any sections. One of the reasons I believe in this method is that it forces me to teach passages such as Hebrews 6 that I would never choose to teach otherwise. If I only teach the sections of Scripture that I prefer and which are easy to interpret, I do God's word a disservice, and I myself never study the difficult passages.

I not only believe in teaching the word expositionally, I also believe that God has gifted me to do so—that for reasons unbeknownst to me, he has given me a capacity to understand and communicate his word for the benefit of others. I trust not the gift but the giver of the gift, so I do what I am gifted to do with confidence that God will be there when I study and teach, even when I study and teach Hebrews 6.

When the day came, I tore into the text. After a while, I felt I had a better understanding of it—that it was not, in fact, teaching that believers could forfeit their salvation. But one phrase plagued me. The writer says that it is impossible for those who fall away from God to "be brought back to repentance."

If it's impossible for them to repent again, that means they must have at one time repented, right? That means they must have at one time been saved, right? And if they had once been saved and have now fallen away and cannot repent again, they have forfeited their salvation, right? These questions haunted me. I prayed at several points during my study, asking God to illuminate the text for me.

Then one day I walked downtown. On the way, I thought about the text. I ended up contemplating the word "repent." And then, out of nowhere, the word "believe" came to mind. Repent. Believe. Repent and believe!

I remembered that Jesus said, "The kingdom of God is near. Repent and believe the good news" (Mark 1:15). I remembered some verses in Acts where repentance is seen as only the beginning of the conversion process and faith is seen as the end (Acts 19:4, 20:21, 26:20). And then I remembered that the writer of Hebrews, only a few verses earlier, wrote of "repentance from acts that lead to death, and of faith in God" (Hebrews 6:1).

These people the writer speaks of in verses 4 through 8 hadn't believed, I reasoned; they had only repented. They had turned away from their previous beliefs to join the community of God, but they ultimately rejected God's good news.

I don't know if it was God who called to my mind the words "repent and believe" that day I walked downtown, but I think it may have been. I make no claim that my interpretations are God-inspired, for I have no doubt that some of them have been incorrect. But perhaps it was God's way of honoring his word and his gift. Whatever it was, I was encouraged to continue studying and teaching the difficult parts of his word. That courage, I believe, is from God.

TURNING FORTY

It was one comment among many on the occasion of my fortieth birthday. When it was made, I thought nothing of it. Later that evening, as I shared with God my reflections about turning forty, it resurfaced, and I immediately connected it with an image that appeared in my mind almost two years earlier. The image was the bride of Christ.

On the first Saturday morning of December in 1995, two years earlier, I hung up the phone, knowing that the relationship I had assumed would lead to marriage was over. So I got in my car and spent that day with God. I ended up walking among the redwoods, and in the middle of my despair, hope filled my thoughts. I somehow knew that God would bring life out of death. I pondered a new course, but what would it be?

God's call to husbands in Ephesians 5:25 is to lay down their lives for their wives. It had become clear that I would have no wife, at least not in the near future, but I still had the desire to lay down my life for something, for someone, for some . . . woman. Perhaps it is a desire that God has woven into the heart of every man. Then the image began to take shape—the image of the bride. The church, according to Ephesians 5 and Revelation 19:7, is the bride of Christ. Yes, that was the course. I sensed God saying something like, "There she is; lay down your life for her."

Within a few days, I knew what I wanted to do. I wanted to start a ministry for young adults, to teach them the Scriptures in the framework of a community, to help them draw close to Jesus. So that December, I prayed. In January and February 1996,

I asked a few people to join me. In March, we prayed together. In April, we started the Young Adults Fellowship.

On October 19, 1997, the Young Adults Fellowship threw me a fortieth birthday party. The party was breaking up as one of the men in the fellowship approached me. He surveyed the twenty or so remaining people and observed, "Scott, you've created a family here." I said thank you and forgot about it—until later that evening.

"Scott, you've created a family here." Those words from earlier in the day resurfaced and hung in my mind.

"There she is; lay down your life for her." Those words from two years earlier resurfaced and joined with the words from earlier in the day.

First, as I tried to come to grips with the loss of a cherished relationship, God filled me with hope by telling me to lay down my life for the bride of Christ. Then, when the fortieth birthday of a single man might give him pause to question whether he'd missed something along the way, God flooded my heart with joy by showing me a family. I laid down my life for the bride of Christ, and God created a family.

THE HAND OF HEAVEN

In the middle of my journey northward, I stopped to peer into the blue of the Pacific. It seemed to have what I wanted. I wanted to be healed from the past and liberated to enter the present. I wanted freedom as vast as the ocean. So when I arrived at my destination, a retreat center north of the Bay, I knew that I would be searching for healing.

At 11:00 a.m., I entered my assigned room, perched like an eagle's nest atop an old Episcopalian church. The steeple and the wooden cross on top of it were outside the window, directly in front of me. I knelt in my room, offering up the next twenty-four hours to God. As I fixed my gaze on the cross, these words took shape in my mind: "You will find healing in my cross."

I contemplated those words for the first few hours. Then I read Matthew's account of the crucifixion, which inspired me to recall Isaiah 53:5: "by his wounds we are healed." For the rest of the day, until I went to sleep, I prayed and meditated over those words, repeating them to myself countless times and dwelling on Christ's love for me as demonstrated in his wounds.

I thought I would spend the rest of my time contemplating those words, but by the time I awoke, new words had settled into my consciousness: "You cannot heal yourself." I cling fiercely to the belief that I can analyze my way to spiritual health. But I knew I had to embrace my powerlessness. As I tried to do so, I remembered these words from Exodus 15:26: "for I am the Lord, who heals you." I cannot heal myself, but the Lord heals. He does heal! But will he heal me?

I wondered. The sun began its morning ascent and peeked through the trees. As soon as I saw the rising sun, a treasured verse committed to memory long ago ascended in my thoughts: "But for you who revere my name, the sun of righteousness will rise with healing in its wings. And you will go out and leap like calves released from the stall" (Malachi 4:2). Yes, the sun *will* rise! I *will* go out and leap! I will be healed; I will be free. As the sun continued to rise, its rays, like wings from heaven, pointed to the cross outside my room. The sun had risen, with healing in its wings.

At 11:00 a.m., I finished where I had started twenty-four hours earlier: on my knees, in prayer, eyes on the cross. The sun had risen above the trees and flooded the room with light. At the conclusion of my prayer, I dropped my head in weariness. What I saw next startled me. The sunlight, playing with the frame of the window, had created a shadow on my shirt. The image was unmistakable. It was the cross. Only this time, it wasn't outside the room and in front of me, it was inside the room and next to me, even on me.

"You will find healing in my cross." The hand of heaven had pointed to the cross and then painted a picture of it on my chest. The healer had drawn near and applied the instrument of his wounds to my body. By his wounds he was healing me. And I would be free, like a calf from the stall—like the blue of the Pacific.

A RACE FOR HEROES

I have wondered about my recreational choices. I like golf and fly-fishing, two difficult and often frustrating avocations. I have wondered what attracts me to such endeavors. Why, when I want to get away from it all, do I take on something that it's well nigh impossible to do well?

The municipal golf courses I play tend to be forgiving, with wide fairways and little rough. Even on such courses, I seldom come close to breaking eighty. The privately owned courses I play are more challenging. Naturally, I prefer them, even though they usually trounce me.

After a particularly rough round at a private course, I lamented to a playing partner, "Why is it that the best golf courses are always so difficult?" He quickly responded, "And why is it that you fish for twenty-inch wild trout instead of ten-inch hatchery trout?" I knew the answer: I like a challenge.

Something tells me I was born liking a challenge. The evidence around me suggests that I am not alone. Most people, it seems, crave a challenge. If it's too easy, it's not interesting. Children relish heroic stories of adventure. Invariably, such stories feature threats that must be overcome. Back then, my first daughter wanted me to tell her stories but wouldn't let me finish until "something bad happened."

We all start out wanting to live heroically, for something beyond ourselves. Then something bad happens. Things happen to us that shouldn't happen. People say and do things they shouldn't say and do. We feel pain and shame and despair. Sometimes it seems to take all our resources just to survive, let alone live heroically. We wonder if the good guys really do win in the end.

Something tells me not only that I was born liking a challenge but also that I was born *for* a challenge—and for something more significant than shooting low scores and catching wild trout.

The writer of Hebrews sees life itself as a challenge. He sees it as a race fraught with hindrances and entanglements that can cause loss of heart. Yet he holds out hope that it can and should be lived heroically. In Hebrews 12:1-3, he challenges us to believe and act on the promises of God, running the race of faith without being deterred by the pain it causes.

Many have run the race before us, he says. In a sense, they're in the stands. They are not literally watching us but are, in a metaphorical sense, cheering us on through the stories of their lives as recorded in the Old Testament and Hebrews 11. "Trust the Lord!" they shout. "The promises are worth waiting for! You can do it! Keep going!" The writer singles out one hero in particular: "Let us fix our eyes on Jesus, the author and perfecter of our faith, who for the joy set before him endured the cross, scorning its shame, and sat down at the right hand of the throne of God. Consider him who endured such opposition form sinful men, so that you will not grow weary and lose heart."

Opposition and the shame of the cross did not keep Jesus from running the race. Instead, he believed the promises of God, looking forward to the joy of reigning for the sake of good in God's new creation.

What do I learn from Jesus? I learn that the life of faith is hard but that joy is set before us. Jesus took his seat on a throne at the right hand of God, and so will his followers (Revelation

3:21, 22:5). Our destiny as men and women—to reign with the Lord Jesus Christ in God's new creation—will be fulfilled.

I must not live in denial. I must allow myself to feel what I feel, including pain, despair, and shame. Nevertheless, I can't drop out of the race because of such feelings. I must keep believing the promises of God. If I do grow weary, I can fix my eyes on Jesus, who rejuvenates me by virtue of how he ran and where he finished. He assures me that there is still a place for heroes, and that the good guys really do win in the end.

The writer of Hebrews invites us to use our imaginations and picture a scene like this:

You're in the stadium, running the race. It's been a hard race, and you're exhausted. The stands are filled with the likes of Abel and Enoch and Noah and Abraham and Sarah and Isaac and Jacob and Joseph and Moses and Rahab and countless others. When they see you, they cheer you on. You draw strength from their encouragement, and you keep moving forward.

In the distance, you see another figure—one who's not seated in the stands with the other veterans but who's waiting at what looks to be the finish line. There is a finish line! As you keep running, you see him more clearly—so clearly that you can somehow look into his soul. This one, you know, is like no other. No one has run the race as he has. As deafening as the crowd noise is, you hear his voice above all others. Cheers and encouragement pour out from his soul, from the race he ran. You decide you want to fix your eyes on him. The race is still hard—maybe it's harder than ever—but there's something about that man at the finish line. You sense that when you get to where he is, all will be well, and that you will know joy as you never have. As you get closer, you can't wait to see his face.

Finally, you cross the finish line and collapse into his arms. He embraces you. Now he fixes his eyes on you. He says, "I've been waiting for this day since before time began. I've been waiting for *you* since before time began. I'm so pleased with you. You ran so well. Let me tell you about my kingdom. I want to share it with you. Let me show you around."

THE LIGHT GIVER

I planned to meditate on three passages of Scripture in my favorite room at a retreat house in Point Reyes. When I arrived, I discovered that my room assignment had been changed. The room I wanted provides a panoramic view of the Tomales Bay and the tree-covered hills. During daylight hours, the sun fills the room with light. The room I was given hugs the hills and, with a small window above head level, provides no view at all. Only a few rays of sunlight find their way into it.

Nevertheless, I was not disappointed. It was the fourth straight year I had taken such a retreat, and I had learned to trust the Lord with it. Two years earlier, I didn't get my favorite room, either, and at first I was disappointed. Back then, as I settled into the room I didn't want, I sensed the Lord telling me that I was in a different place spiritually from the previous year. The Lord put me in a different place to show me that I was in a different "place." So this time, I simply shrugged my shoulders and thought, "I wonder what the Lord has for me in this room."

Upon entering my room, I immediately noticed an icon. It was a picture of Jesus, who was labeled "The Light Giver." As I evaluated the room, the best position had me pointed in the direction of the icon. I read, pondered, and prayed my way through the passages I had selected. Mostly, I stuck to my agenda, but every time I looked up, the icon was looking back at me. The title for Jesus intrigued me: The Light Giver.

Finally, during the last hour of my retreat, I asked the Lord, "Are you telling me something?" A few moments later, I remembered that throughout this retreat, and even on the way to it,

I had been particularly impacted by light—the sun peeking through the fog, the dew-covered leaves reflecting the sunlight, the rising mist making the rays of the sun visible, the vapor of my breath being captured by the morning sun. Soon after arriving, I had taken comfort in the thought that though the light did not fill my room, the Light Giver fills me no matter the place.

Before leaving, I took one last walk around the grounds. At that moment I felt these words in my spirit: "Scott, you, too, are a light giver." Were they from God?

I had been a pastor for four years. Before that, for eleven years, I was a journalist. I knew how to be a journalist. Sometimes I wasn't sure how to be a pastor. But I was sure of one thing: I wanted to teach the Scriptures in a way that revealed God, particularly as he is revealed in Jesus Christ, so that people might know him and worship him. Isn't that giving light? Still, it seemed presumptuous to think of myself as a light giver. After all, I had just spent two days staring at an icon that proclaimed Jesus to be *the* light giver.

I returned home, and to prepare for a class I would be teaching, I started to read 2 Corinthians. I arrived at 2 Corinthians 4:6: "For God, who said, 'Light shall shine out of darkness,' is the One who has shone in our hearts to give the Light of the knowledge of the glory of God in the face of Christ" (New American Standard Bible). The apostle Paul was writing about what happened in the hearts of the apostles so that they were able share God with others. Give the light. Of the knowledge of the glory of God. In the face of Christ. That's exactly what I wanted to do.

Through sunlight that continually and variously piqued my interest, a switched room assignment, a little icon, and a verse of Scripture, I concluded that God was telling me, "Scott, that's exactly what I want you to do."

The teacher and the student

It was a fellowship meal. My friend John was sitting at a table by himself, so I joined him. John has mental and physical disabilities that slow him down a bit, but his heart is soft toward God. He often makes unpretentious yet insightful observations.

Some years earlier, John had approached me with a question that troubled him. He wondered whether he was a "real Christian." I was convinced of the genuineness of John's faith. We talked on a few occasions, and at some point John was able to put the question to rest.

When I sat next to him this time, I asked him what the Lord had been showing him. He answered, as he always does, with revealing honesty. I knew what was coming next. You can't ask John to tell you something about himself without his asking the same question in return.

"What's the Lord been showing you, Scott?"

I knew that a standard answer wouldn't suffice. "Well, John, I think I've been doubting God's love for me, and I think he's been trying to show me how much he loves me."

A look of shock came over John's face. "But Scott, that's what you taught me! You taught me that God loves me! That's what you taught me!"

Hmmm.

Well, if John says so, I suppose I did teach him that, but when it comes to my understanding of God's love for me, it slips away from me sometimes. But I think God sent me to John's table so that this time, my friend could teach me. First, I taught John that God loves him. A few years later, John taught me that God loves me.

The apostle Paul says that the church constitutes the body of Christ. Christ's body is no longer on earth, but he makes his presence known through his people. Each person in his church has a valuable and unique contribution to make. Paul goes so far as to say that "those parts of the body that seem to be weaker are indispensable" (1 Corinthians 12:22).

Someone who teaches me about God's love, I should say, is indispensable.

Runny noses and open wounds

The prospect of spending a day at an orphanage in Belize gladdened me. I enjoy children, and I hoped, along with two friends, to give these little ones some much-needed affection, at least for a day. When we arrived, the children mobbed us. They were perhaps a little more starved for attention than I thought they would be, but for the most part, everything was as I expected.

Except, that is, for the runny noses and open wounds. Oh, if I had given it any thought, what else should I have expected? This was an orphanage in a Third World country. The site of runny noses and open wounds meant one thing to me: disease.

Suddenly, the prospect of spending a day at this place troubled me. For the first thirty minutes or so, I did my best to keep the children at arm's length, fearing that too much touching would put me at risk of illness. I wanted to be healthy for the rest of our missions trip.

Trinidad, a particularly rambunctious five-year-old boy, was bouncing on my knee. I made sure he got no closer than my knee. As he bounced there, I considered Jesus. I remembered the beating he took for my sin—for my sickness. I considered that he embraced my sickness and absorbed it into his body. I remembered that by his wounds I was healed. I remembered Isaiah 53:5: "But he was pierced for our transgressions, / He was crushed for our iniquities; / The punishment that brought us peace was upon him, / And by his wounds we are healed."

Immediately, I grabbed the little boy with both hands and pulled him to me. With one hand I embraced his back and with

65

the other I cradled his head. I held him against my chest. I kept holding him there. The boy, who had earlier seemed unhappy unless he was bouncing into something, rested peacefully in my arms. I don't know how long I held him; I only know that I held him for a long time—that I wanted to hold him for a long time. From then on, I wanted to hold all the children.

I remember thinking, as I watched Trinidad bouncing on my knee, that I wanted to be like Jesus. I wanted my hug to heal this little boy of abandonment, neglect, and loneliness. I wanted to be to Trinidad what Jesus was to me. For those few moments, as our bodies rested against each other, I didn't care whether I became sick.

The next day, I came down with a cold. It didn't matter.

PINCHED NERVE

I had come to Belize with a dozen others from our church to build a community center for a village of refugees. I had also come with prayers that I would be able to encourage local pastors. We arrived at the work site the first day, but I couldn't work because of a pinched nerve in my neck.

Depressed because I was unable to contribute, I trudged to the side of the dirt road and asked the Lord, "What do I do now?" Just then a passer-by came into view. He was walking along the road, and he stopped because he was curious about the construction project. He approached me to inquire about it.

His name was Shu. He was a Mayan, probably in his seventies, no more than four and one-half feet tall. I told him that we came from a church in the United States.

"I'm a pastor," he said.

My depression lifted.

Shu was on his way to pick a bagful of oranges from his family grove, which was a mile away. He invited me to accompany him. We shared stories as we walked together. I enjoyed his company, and he evidently enjoyed mine, for he asked me to join him for the two-mile trip back to his hut. By the time we arrived, he was weary, but he offered me some tea before settling into his hammock. Walking, talking, drinking—we spent the afternoon together.

I couldn't call up any words to encourage him with, but my presence reminded him of a time long ago, when another visitor from the States shared the gospel with him. Shu began to follow Jesus back then, and to lead a small church. When I met him, he was still leading the church. My presence, not my words, encouraged him.

I came to another country to work, but I also came to encourage local pastors with words of wisdom. I was depressed because I couldn't work. Out of nowhere, God sent me a pastor to encourage. I could speak, but what I said didn't matter. In the end, God, and a little Mayan pastor, encouraged me.

When the angel of the Lord called Abraham, he responded, "Here am I." Moses and the prophet Isaiah responded in like manner when heaven came calling (Genesis 22:1, Exodus 3:4, Isaiah 6:8). These and others made themselves available to the Lord, who then gave them an assignment. Isaiah said yes to the assignment even before he knew what it was.

More often than not, my availability—and my presence— is enough.

The stuff that dreams are made of

Once, I think, God spoke to me in a dream.

Sitting on a porch in the country of Belize one evening during a short-term missions trip, I watched two of my friends, Ginny and Ed, walk away together. Wistfully, I turned to another friend, who was sharing the porch with me, and said, "I hope Ginny comes to know the Lord."

Three years earlier, Ginny had come to our church because she wanted to make a fresh start after moving to California from New York. "I decided I needed to start going to church," she said. She began listening to the teaching, singing the songs, and observing all things closely. But she couldn't bring herself to make a commitment to Christ. She decided to join the trip to Belize because she wanted to see what a missions trip was like. She also hoped that what she experienced on the trip would give her the strength to leave an old way of life and begin a new way of life centered on Christ.

Shortly after watching Ginny and Ed walk away, I went to bed. In a dream, I heard that a terrorist was planning an attack in a shopping center. I knew that Ginny was staying in an upstairs apartment behind the shopping center. I sprinted to the apartment, ran up the stairs, and yelled, "Ginny! Ginny! Ginny!" I grabbed her by the hand, and we ran down the stairs to safety. Then I woke up.

The next morning I shared the dream with a few people, including Ginny, but didn't think much of it. Later that morning, Ginny approached me with a curious smile on her face. "Would you baptize me today?" she asked. She told me that she had prayed, in the presence of Ed, after the two of them walked away the previous night, to give her life to Christ.

Later that afternoon, Ginny stood in the cool waters of Jaguar Creek. Flanked by Ed and me, she announced to the group that she had given her life to Christ and that she wanted to be baptized. Baptism symbolizes death and resurrection—death to one way of life and entry into another a way of life. She told us how everyone's care for her had changed her life. After her profession, Ed and I let Ginny fall gently backward into the creek, and the water engulfed her. Then we pulled her out of the water—just as I, in my dream, had pulled her out of her apartment the previous night.

Yanking Ginny out of a dangerous situation one day, albeit in a dream, and pulling her out of water that symbolizes death the next—a coincidence? I don't think so. I think God gave me a picture of what our church did for Ginny.

For three years she had been surrounded by new friends who loved her. They had offered up countless prayers in her behalf. God used those friends, that love, and those prayers to lead Ginny to a new way of life—an eternal way. The people who loved Ginny were given the privilege of taking her by the hand and escorting her into the kingdom of God.

God-given dreams and visions in the Scriptures offer heavenly insight into earthly scenes. For example, the prophet Daniel saw beyond the threats of his day and into the way things are (Daniel 7-8). When Ginny and Ed walked away together, I didn't know what was happening. When I went to sleep, I saw what was really going on.

A NIGHT IN THE VILLAGE

I spent the night with a family of five who lived in a thatched-roof hut. They were Mayans, refugees from Guatemala, but they had been living in a village in Belize for some time. I had come to Belize with a dozen other Americans to help build a community center for the village. The organizers of our trip thought we'd profit from spending a night in the village.

Each of us was assigned a family. Mine consisted of a husband and wife, both about thirty, and their three children. They spoke no English. My Spanish classes from high school came back to me enough so that we could communicate on a rudimentary level. I didn't need to understand them perfectly to see that they enjoyed themselves. Life was hard, but they had each other. They were content.

The woman burned some wood and cooked tortillas and soup over the stove. I played with the children and conversed with the man as best I could. Come nighttime, they fetched a hammock from some neighbors and strung it up for me inside the tiny hut. For them, a hammock was a luxury they couldn't afford. All five of them slept on boards.

Luxury or no, I was uncomfortable and couldn't sleep, which turned out to be a good thing, for I was awake when the man arose, walked over to the wall, and pulled down a machete. He shuffled out the door and left for work. I looked at my watch. It was 3:30 a.m.

The man worked the fields, picking fruit for pay to provide for his family. Some days, the field was a short distance away. Other days, like this one, he had to hike several miles just to get to work.

I've thought of that man often. Is it a good day if he picks lots of fruit? Are oranges better than bananas? Are bananas better than oranges? If he picks more fruit than his co-worker, does he feel better about himself?

I don't envision him fretting over such questions. We fret over them where I live, though. We want to feel good about ourselves. In order to do so, we count and compare. When the counting's done, and you've got more than I do, or you sell more than I do, or you're catching up to me, I question my value. Problem is, there's always someone who's got more, who's selling more, or who's catching up.

John the Baptist told some soldiers to be content with their pay (Luke 3:14). The writer of Hebrews advises us to be content with what we have because God has said, "Never will I leave you; never will I forsake you" (Hebrews 13:5). The apostle Paul said that his contentment comes from knowing Christ, that the Spirit strengthens him to know Christ, and that he has learned to be content whatever the circumstances (Philippians 3:4-11, 4:11-13; Ephesians 3:14-19). He also wrote, "But if we have food and clothing, we will be content with that" (1 Timothy 6:8).

I wish I could feel good just because God loves me and Christ died for me. In other words, I wish I didn't care how I felt about myself, only how God feels about me. Most days I'm fine. Other days I fret.

I've learned much about contentment from studying the Scriptures. I've also learned from a Mayan farm worker in Belize. The organizers who thought we'd profit from spending a night in the village? In my case, they were right.

Chapter 3

TENDING GOD'S GARDEN IN SEARCH OF A WOMAN

ONE FOR THE AGES

How does a man find a wife? I wanted to know because I wanted to find one, particularly as I drew closer to my forties as a single man. I didn't feel like going out of my way to look for a wife because doing so would take time away from my passions, especially pastoral work.

How did the first man find a wife? God created a garden and told the man to cultivate it—a task that must have delighted him. But Adam was alone with his passions, a state that even God himself decried. God proposed a solution, but first he made the man name animals. Adam saw lots of creatures but not one woman. Finally, God fashioned a woman and brought her to the man. Adam responded with eagerness (Genesis 2:15-25).

I saw myself in the first man. I was cultivating my garden, the church, but I was alone with my passions. I saw lots of women, and pursued a few of them, but none was the woman for me. If the first man didn't need to leave his garden to find a wife, I concluded that I could stay in mine.

Inspired by the Genesis story, I began to pray in a new way: "Lord, you bring her to me. I'll respond, but you bring her to me."

I went about my routine, cultivating my garden, but I became more watchful. On a few occasions, I thought God was bringing a woman to me. I responded—I moved toward each woman—but nothing developed. I was naming animals, it seemed: waiting, losing hope, getting older. Still, I prayed, and I watched.

One Sunday evening, I was watching our people at a worship service. I watched one woman in particular. I suppose I should have been worshiping, but, well, she was beautiful. I wanted to meet her. At the conclusion of the service, she was conversing with others. I started to join their circle but stopped because I felt frantic. At that point, trusting God meant backing away. "If it's right for us to meet," I told myself, "we'll meet."

So I tended to the garden: I spent time with others in the church. Thirty minutes passed. When my last conversation ended, I turned toward the refreshment table. Standing in my way—all by herself—was the woman I wanted to meet.

I responded.

We spoke for twenty minutes. She was not only beautiful, she was also bright and intriguing. We parted, but we would speak a few weeks later, and again, a few weeks after that. The third time we spoke, I invited Karen to lunch: my first date with the woman who would be my wife.

Turns out the Genesis story was my story.

Perhaps it's every couple's story. I use it in premarital counseling, and every couple I've met with has identified with it. When the author of Genesis told the story of the first couple, he gave us one for the ages.

The napkins

When Don and I started meeting weekly for coffee at 7:00 a.m., we mostly commiserated with each other. He was trying to rebuild a house, but it was taking forever. I was trying to prop up a relationship, but it was falling apart.

One morning, I reported that the relationship had collapsed and he reported that the remodel had stalled again. For an hour, we lamented harder than usual. After he excused himself to go to the restroom, I grabbed a cocktail napkin, scribbled on it, and placed it on the table. When Don returned, this message was waiting for him: "It's gonna work! P.S. I don't know how it's gonna work. November 29, 1995." I felt sure that his story would have a good ending. I wasn't so sure about my story.

Later, I excused myself, which gave Don time to scribble a note of his own. When I returned, a cocktail napkin was waiting for me with the same message. He felt sure that my story would have a good ending. I came to work that day and pinned the napkin that Don had given me to the wall. I looked at it again. "It's gonna work!" I hoped.

Don and I continued meeting together for four more years. We had been buddies as carefree teenagers, but as burdened thirty-somethings, our friendship deepened.

He finished the house, but he and his wife dreamed of moving to the Central Coast. I was still looking for a wife.

One morning, he told me the news: he found a job and a piece of land on the Central Coast. He'd be moving in a few months. So on a Monday morning, in the fall of 1999, we met for our last weekly session. I brought with me the napkin he had given me four years earlier and showed it to him.

His story had a good ending. He sold his house and made enough money off it to build a house on the Central Coast, this time through a contractor. After living in temporary housing, he and his family moved in a year later. He told me our weekly meetings had inspired him to follow his heart.

I would miss Don. All told, our weekly meetings spanned five years. During that time I suffered other relational heartaches. I shared them all with Don, who received everything with compassion.

At our last meeting, I had some news for him. Later that day, I'd be having lunch with a woman whom I had just met. I didn't know much about Karen, but I was trying to be hopeful.

The lunch went well—well enough that more dates followed, and a proposal, and a wedding. Turns out my last meeting with my old friend took place on the same day as my first date with my future wife. Don had carried me from a broken relationship to a lasting one. He also stood beside me as my best man.

The napkins were right. It worked—for both of us.

The apostle Paul writes, "And we know that in all things God works for the good of those who love him, who have been called according to his purpose" (Romans 8:28). Taken in isolation, the verse makes us wonder: what is "the good?" In context, "the good" is the completion of God's plan to raise from the dead those who love him and to restore them as his image bearers so that they perfectly reflect his glory and reign over his renewed creation with wisdom. God uses everything that happens to believers in Christ, particularly suffering, to bring about this good purpose. It's gonna work.

Until the final day, we have no guarantees that it's gonna work according to our conception of good. But if the story has a good ending, maybe God also writes good endings to some of our chapters to give us hope for the future. If so, I think the tale of the napkins was such a chapter.

Okay to Go

Upon the recommendation of a friend, in the summer of 1997, I went to see the movie *Contact*. Not very often have I gone to a movie theater by myself, but this was one of those occasions.

One scene caught my attention for its portrayal of courage. The character played by Jodi Foster is in the cockpit of a kind of space ship. It looks as if the ship is on the verge of breaking apart, and Foster's character, who has lost contact with those in the control tower, assumes that they are on the verge of aborting the mission. She tries to communicate to the leaders that she wants to continue the mission, even though it looks as if she might be killed. She desperately speaks into her headset, hoping someone will hear, "Okay to go! Okay to go! Okay to go!"[5]

That scene lingered in my mind as I left the theater. I went for a walk in Memorial Park, across the street. I walked around the duck ponds and through the open-air amphitheater.

I was thirty-nine years old that summer. I had been single all my life and, for the most part, content. But a few years earlier, I had begun to feel a deep desire for a wife that only intensified as time went on.

The words "okay to go" echoed in my mind. Somehow, I connected those words to my status. I made those words my own and turned them into a prayer. In walking with God for so many years, and in wrestling with him over my desire to be married, I had come to more fully trust him with my longings. With tears flowing, I told the Lord, "If you want me to be single, okay to go."

Some teach that it is important to believe that God will give you what you want. I think it's important to believe that God knows what you need better than you do. Facing the prospect of crucifixion, Jesus prayed, "*Abba*, Father, everything is possible for you. Take this cup from me. Yet not what I will, but what you will" (Mark 14:36). Jesus trusted the Father, and the Father didn't remove the cup.

Two summers after my walk in the park, I met a woman. We went to lunch, and I felt a connection. Her interests included hiking and Shakespeare. We made plans to go for a hike the next Saturday. The day after our lunch, I read the morning paper while eating breakfast. The entertainment section featured a story about a free "Shakespeare in the Park" performance of *A Comedy of Errors* that Saturday night.

Later that morning, I went for a walk, and it struck me: the location of the upcoming Shakespeare performance was Memorial Park, the same park I walked through after seeing *Contact* two years earlier.

I asked Karen if she would like to cap off the hike with Shakespeare. She said yes. After our hike, we enjoyed the performance together, in the same spot where I offered up my "okay to go" prayer two years earlier.

In the coming months, Karen and I continued to spend time together and felt more drawn to each other. Six months after our first date, we were engaged. A year later, we were married.

I told God, "Okay to go"—meaning, it was okay if he wanted me to be single. Two years later, God told me, "Okay to go"—meaning, it was okay to get married.

I don't mean to say that when the location of the Shakespeare performance dawned on me that I knew that God was leading me to marry Karen. I've seen similar coincidences turn into nothing. It took months of prayer and time together to sense God's leading. But in retrospect, and it's often in retrospect that these things become more clear, I do think that God was encouraging me to move toward Karen and that he chose to encourage me in a poetic way that would delight my heart.

Come to the Quiet

For several years, my usual Saturday-morning routine was to walk to a downtown bakery and spend a few hours with a cup of coffee, the newspaper, and my thoughts. One Saturday morning in early November, I came across a story in the newspaper that featured the Mount Angel Abbey in Mount Angel, Oregon.

The photograph in the paper looked familiar, and I realized that I had visited this place before. About ten years earlier, in the course of visiting some friends in Oregon, I called another friend who was living nearby. This friend wanted to show me the Mount Angel Abbey. She had spent some time there and had become acquainted with some of the monks. This place and these people were special, she said. When she visited, she felt at peace. When I visited with her, I could understand what she was talking about. We wandered the grounds and talked with some of the monks. I, too, felt at peace.

As I read the newspaper story at my table in the bakery, I felt drawn to this place again. I don't usually make many spontaneous decisions, but something told me I should visit the Mount Angel Abbey again. So immediately, I called Ken and Laurie, the friends I had visited earlier, and asked if their standing invitation to join them any time for Thanksgiving was still good. Some years ago, I had visited them for Thanksgiving and was nourished by their friendship. When I called this time, they were happy to receive me again.

When I traveled to Oregon, I was seeking direction. I had met a woman named Karen, and we were moving closer together. Because of past disappointments, I was afraid of marriage.

83

Karen was a quiet person. As a quiet person myself, I thought maybe I would do better with someone who was more outgoing. I wondered if I would hear from God at the Mount Angel Abbey. After all, he seemed to be sending me there.

When I arrived in Oregon, I told Ken that at some point during my stay, I'd like to spend two hours at the Mount Angel Abbey. Ken's father-in-law Ron wanted to come along, so the three of us headed for the abbey. We split up and each spent two hours on our own. I ended up in a small prayer chapel, alone with God, my thoughts, and my prayers. Once again, I felt at peace. But I sensed no direction.

That night, Laurie's parents joined us for dinner. Ron announced that during his time at the abbey, he had purchased an album by John Michael Talbot, and we listened to the music during dinner. Several people expressed their fondness for it. I remembered how his music had seen me through a difficult season in my life.

I returned home, refreshed by my time in Oregon but no less afraid of marriage. When I entered my house, I noticed a plastic CD case on the couch. My housemate had placed the disc in the CD player and left the case there. It was a John Michael Talbot album. "What is it with these John Michael Talbot albums?" I wondered. Immediately, I remembered the title of the album Ron purchased: *Come to the Quiet*. I remembered my question about Karen's quiet nature. Could it be that God sent me to another state and back again to hear and understand the message "Come to the Quiet"?

After I returned from Oregon, I continued moving through my fears and toward Karen. Two months later we were engaged, and six months after that we were married. In the quietness of her soul, I have found rest. Sometimes, when I find myself over-wrought by the cares of life, I allow myself to hear those words again, "Come to the Quiet," and I return to Karen. She has been my abbey.

The biblical narratives are full of stories in which God sends the players of the drama here and there in order that people might hear from him. While Cornelius, an Italian soldier, was praying in Caesarea, an angel appeared to him in a vision and told him to send for a man named Peter, an apostle of Jesus. The next day in Joppa, Peter had a vision, after which the Holy Spirit told him to go with three men who were looking for him. Peter followed the men to Caesarea, where he entered the house of Cornelius. The apostle told the soldier and those gathered with him about Jesus. They believed what he said and were baptized (Acts 10).

God arranges for us to hear from him. Usually, we don't get a "sign." I don't think "Come to the Quiet" was a message from God that I should marry Karen. It may have been, perhaps, a nudge.

If we attend closely to the stories of our lives, we'll observe themes, patterns, and connections. Perhaps we'll also feel an occasional nudge from someone who's trying to get our attention.

INNER HEALING PRAYER

I wanted to be married. I prayed fervently for a wife. Then Karen entered my life. She was bright, beautiful, and stable—and she wanted to be with me. God answered my prayers. Or so it seemed.

At first, I rejoiced. Then I trembled. I started getting anxious about what comes with marriage: commitment, intimacy, and exposure. I had reasons for my fears, mostly related to old wounds. Although they were reasonable, they were also useful: they protected me from the unknown.

I went for long, prayer-filled walks to send my fears away, but they wouldn't leave. On one of those walks, I came upon a member of my church. Richard was sitting outside a café, sipping some coffee, and soaking in the mid-autumn sun. We knew of each other, but we had not met.

"I see you walking around," he said. (Oh, people were watching?) "That's what I used to do when I was single." We shared our stories. Like me, Richard had harbored fears about marriage. So, how did he overcome them?

"Inner healing prayer," he said.

He described long stretches during which friends would pray over him for emotional healing. God responded to those prayers, he said, and helped him move toward marriage.

I remembered my longtime friends, Tom and Mary Jane, who had come to my side at anxious junctures in my life: after a breakup, when I lost a job, when my mother was dying. When I got home, I called them. I told them of my fears and asked if they would pray for me. They invited me over, and they prayed for me long into the night.

Their prayers didn't heal the old wounds that night, nor did they send the fears away. But now I was no longer praying alone. And I was strengthened to move toward Karen despite my fears. Three months later, I proposed, and nine months later, I married her—not without fear in either case. But I decided not to capitulate to fear. That's courage, isn't it? Courage isn't the absence of fear; courage is doing what frightens you.

"Be strong and courageous," God told Joshua. Why? "For the Lord your God will be with you wherever you go" (Joshua 1:9). He'll hear you. He'll lead you. He'll strengthen you.

He was with me when I met Richard. He was with me when I visited Tom and Mary Jane. He was with me when I proposed to Karen. He was with me when I married her. He's with me still.

THE VOICE OF PEBBLE BEACH

As I stood on the eighteenth tee at the Pebble Beach Golf Links, I was conflicted. On the one hand, I wanted to take in the scene. After all, this was probably the only time I would play what many consider the greatest golf course in the world. I had never even hoped to play it because the greens fees are so expensive, but some generous friends had given me a round of golf there as a gift. Of all the storied holes at Pebble Beach, the eighteenth is the most famous. Naturally, I wanted to capture the moment, to appreciate the beauty and history of the place. On the other hand, I wanted to hit a good shot.

Hook it left, and I'm in the Pacific Ocean. Slice it right, and I'm in the houses. The place, the moment, and the difficulty of the shot made me feel a tad nervous. Nervous is not what you want to feel when hitting a golf shot. Hitting a good drive at this time would require mental preparation, I thought.

Yet, I decided that hitting a good drive was not as important as enjoying the moment. As best I could, I pushed thoughts of my upcoming shot out of my mind and concentrated on feeling the vibes of Pebble Beach.

Just as I managed to arrange my thoughts, the voice of a young girl disrupted them. "I found a golf ball," she said. She had seen my foursome waiting on the tee. "Do you want a golf ball?" she said to anyone on the tee who would hear her. "It's a man's golf ball." She was rather insistent.

My internal voices were already dueling for my attention. Now this outside voice was asking to be heard. For an instant, I deemed it an intrusion. I envisioned someone scolding her,

"Don't you know where you are? This is the eighteenth hole at Pebble Beach! This is hallowed ground!" I smiled at how ridiculous such a reprimand would sound. How hardened would one have to be to berate such a child?

Her voice spoke with the clarity of innocence, cutting through the banality of my ruminations. I now knew which voice I needed to hear. It belonged to a little girl. Hitting a good drive wasn't important. Absorbing the aura of Pebble Beach wasn't important. It was important that I appreciate what was really important. What was really important was one of God's children. A little girl found a treasure. What's more important than that?

When Jesus entered the temple, children hailed him as the Messiah, much to the chagrin of the chief priests and teachers of the law. Jesus, evoking Psalm 8:2, told the authorities, "From the lips of children and infants you have ordained praise" (Matthew 21:16). Jesus was saying that God had prepared the children to praise the Messiah. Sometimes children, in their innocence, reflect a better understanding of truth than the experts.

When I played Pebble Beach, I was three weeks away from getting married. Perhaps one day I would have a little girl of my own, I thought. What would be more important then: Daddy's golf game or her treasures?

I didn't have the presence of mind to accept the girl's offer. I didn't turn around to see her face. But I heard her voice, and that seemed to be enough.

I stepped up to the tee and hit a good drive, long and straight.

Three years later, my wife and I had our first child, a girl. Six years later we had our second child, another girl. Sometimes, when my girls want to share their discoveries with me, I hear the voice of the girl from Pebble Beach, who reminds me to listen up.

ACHING FOR BEAUTY

I have a friend who in his forties left his home in Idaho and moved to Romania to care for orphans. When he came to visit me in California, I took him to beautiful places: San Francisco, the beach, the oak-covered hills of the Peninsula. At some point, William mentioned, by contrast, the squalid conditions in Romania.

Finally, we strolled through downtown Palo Alto. I led him into the courtyard of a gorgeous, Mediterranean-styled hotel, the kind that charges four hundred dollars a night. I asked William what he thought of it.

I half expected him to launch into a tirade against Western decadence. Instead, with eyes and voice that conveyed deep longing, he turned to me and said, "Oh, my eyes delight in it."

There is something to be said about the inequity of a world in which some have no home and others pay four hundred dollars a night for a bed. William, no doubt, could speak to the issue with wisdom and experience. This issue, however, did not immediately come to mind when I asked for his reaction to the hotel. Instead, he responded to beauty. Living in the midst of ugliness, William's capacity for appreciating beauty had been deepened.

William, I imagine, could resonate with David, whose unpleasant, even desperate, living conditions aroused in him a desire to dwell in the tabernacle so that he might "gaze upon the beauty of the Lord" (Psalm 27:4). Both the moveable tabernacle and the stationary temple, God's earthly dwellings, were made to be beautiful, with precious materials. When the tabernacle and the temple were finished, God filled each of them with his "glory," his visible presence (Exodus 40:34, 2 Chronicles 7:1). What the people beheld—the beauty of the structures and the glory that filled them—told them something about what they couldn't behold: their God.

We most often use the word "beautiful" in reference to what we perceive with our senses. Sometimes, though, we use it to describe imperceptible attributes, such as character. We can't see God, but if we could, we'd say he was "beautiful," and we would want to gaze upon him.

Is it possible to gaze upon the beauty of the Lord, whom we can't see? The tabernacle and the temple helped the Israelites of old understand the beauty of the Lord. Is there anything that helps us?

Speaking of God's Son, the apostle John writes, "The Word became flesh and made his dwelling among us. We have seen his glory, the glory of the One and Only, who came from the Father, full of grace and truth" (John 1:14). Today, Jesus Christ, the Son of God, is both the tabernacle and the temple. Everything that is beautiful about God dwells in Christ. We can perceive the beauty of the Lord as the Holy Spirit opens the eyes of our hearts so that we might behold Christ in the pages of the Scriptures.

William is not alone in his ache for beauty. Men and women go to great lengths to see or create something beautiful. Why? We must have been created with a capacity for beauty. The ache, if we follow it, will finally lead us to gaze upon our Creator, who gave us his Son.

I think William, as he stood in the courtyard of the hotel, was aching for Christ. I ached with him.

THE HITCHHIKER

Seldom do I pick up a hitchhiker. When I see one, I'll sometimes consider picking him up, but by the time I've finished deliberating with myself, I'm usually a mile down the road, at which point I am able to salve my conscience by concluding that the moment has passed. This approach has protected me from the intrusion of strangers. I had never considered asking God whether he wanted me to pick up a hitchhiker because, I presume, I had been afraid of what he might say.

One day, my usual approach failed me when I decided to consult God.

Every three months, I separate myself from my environment to spend long hours in prayer. When I return, I'm usually more sensitive to my surroundings and to the presence of God. On one such occasion, in a more spiritually sensitive state, I noticed a hitchhiker. As usual, I kept on driving—but I asked God, "Should I pick him up?"

Before I finished my question, God answered it. Or perhaps I answered it; I can't be sure. The three-word answer felt like an intrusion—and a rather violent one at that: "PICK HIM UP!" Although the answer jolted me, I recovered to ask myself (not God) a question: "What should I do now?" If I spent enough time deliberating with myself, I'd be able to put enough distance between the hitchhiker and me that I could convince myself, yet again, that the moment had passed. This time, my conscience wouldn't allow it. Although I was a mile down the road, I made a U-turn and drove back to offer the hitchhiker a ride. But when I returned, he was gone.

If it was God who had instructed me to pick up the hitch-hiker, I was satisfied that I had obeyed him but relieved that nothing more was required of me. Happily, I resumed my journey—only to be interrupted again ten miles down the road. A hitchhiker—the same one—was standing at an intersection, wanting a ride. Another driver had given him a ride to this intersection. I didn't need to pray this time; I just needed to open the door and offer him a ride. He got in.

He told me about his work as a theater critic; I told him that I had visited a local church to pray. He said he had visited that church once, not for spiritual reasons but for a community event. We spoke only briefly. Five miles later, our paths diverged. I let him off at an intersection, where he waited for another ride. The buildup to our encounter seemed ordained, but the encounter itself seemed inconsequential.

Who's to say, however, what's consequential and what isn't? The writer of Hebrews comments: "Do not forget to entertain strangers, for by so doing some people have entertained angels without knowing it" (Hebrews 13:2). Was I entertaining an angel? I can't say for sure that I wasn't.

I think I heard God instruct me to pick him up, but I can't be sure of that, either. I'm sure of this, however: I'd like to trust God enough to ask him more often what I should do, even if it means receiving an inconvenient answer. And, because I believe I'm too cautious, I'd like to follow where the answer leads, even if I only think I'm hearing it.

The dark side of good

I have a theory that goes like this: Most people who think there might be a God do good deeds because they hope to avoid him. They want to do just well enough so that God—if he exists—will keep his nose out of their business and give them a pass at the end. They've convinced themselves that God, if he exists, wants them to be good people and that they're good enough. To think otherwise is to admit they need him.

The standard evangelical approach isn't much better. No one is good enough for God, the line goes, so confess your sins and accept Jesus so that you can go to heaven when you die. The presuppositions are that God wants perfection and that he'll send people to hell for even one sin—unless, of course, they believe in Jesus, in which case he gives them a pass.

But is that what God wants: perfection? I think not. If I'm reading Scriptures right, God isn't interested in obedience; he's interested in obedience from the heart:

- "The sacrifices of God are a broken spirit; a broken and contrite heart, O God, you will not despise" (Psalm 51:17).
- "For you did not receive a spirit that makes you a slave again to fear, but you received the Spirit of sonship. And by him we cry, "*Abba*, Father" (Romans 8:15).

Yes, those who believe in Jesus will be saved, but those who believe in Jesus are indwelt by the Holy Spirit, who revolutionizes their hearts. They will be saved not so much for heaven, it turns out, but for the day heaven comes to earth and remakes it, whereupon they will serve God in his renewed, and eternal, creation. If someone doesn't have the Holy Spirit, he doesn't belong to Christ, he isn't a son of God, and he won't be saved. He cannot please God no matter how good his deeds (Matthew 5:5; Romans 4:1, 8:1-17; Revelation 21:1-4).

God doesn't want people to do good deeds. He wants people to receive his love and to love him in return. He wants people to believe in his Son and receive his Spirit. He wants people to do good deeds *because* they love him. Good deeds, it turns out, can be every bit as sinful as bad deeds. It depends on why you're doing them. Jesus showed the Pharisees that there was a dark side to their good deeds (Matthew 23).

My theory is difficult to believe because most people who do good deeds to avoid God aren't aware of their motives. They really don't want to believe they're trying to avoid God, so they've found ways to deny it. Their motives now reside safely in their subconscious.

I tried my theory out on a stranger. She had overheard a conversation I was having about Jesus with a friend of hers. When I referred to the exclusive claims of Jesus, she jumped in. "Well," she said, "I know a lot of Jews and Muslims and Buddhists who are very beautiful people."

That's when I trotted out my theory. "I don't think God wants good people," I said. "I think most people do good deeds because they're afraid of God and want to avoid him."

She looked angry. I needed to do some more explaining, but she wanted nothing more to do with me.

I don't think my theory is going to be very popular. And maybe I should put it more humbly, if I put it at all.

Changing the world

"We were going to change the world, the six of us."

So began a column in *The Rocky Mountain News*. The columnist, waxing nostalgic after attending the funeral of a college friend, was remembering his days as a journalism student.

His column was particularly interesting to me because I was one of the people he was writing about. I also had attended the funeral, which reunited me with the columnist and three other friends. We gathered to mourn the loss of our friend Sue, who had died of cancer at the age of forty-seven.

"Woodward and Bernstein, who'd inspired us, would be considered mere copy boys compared to what we planned to do," Bill wrote.

A few days after reading Bill's column, I was driving on a highway that I take a few times each year. I glanced to the right to see if my favorite highway sign was still standing. When it first went up, in 1982, it read, "No trucks on Scotts Valley Drive exeeding 6 tons." I was working as a newspaper editor at the time. I noticed that the word "exceeding" was missing the "c," and I assigned a reporter to the story. In response, the Department of Transportation corrected the mistake not by replacing the sign but by attaching a small flap on the existing sign to cover the misspelled word and display the correct spelling.

Yes, the sign was still standing, flap and all. (Finally, the entire sign was replaced in 2010.)

I worked as a journalist for eleven years. Near as I can tell, the closest I came to changing the world was correcting the spelling on a highway sign. But as I read Bill's column, I wasn't thinking of how I didn't change the world. I was thinking of Sue, and of what the six of us shared together as college friends some twenty-five years earlier. I was enjoying the memory of how we *talked about* changing the world.

The Scriptures tell us that God will change the world—literally. He who created the world will one day re-create it. Therefore, the apostle Paul says, those who follow Jesus should realize that they don't toil in vain (1 Corinthians 15:58).

Today, I don't care so much about changing the world. I'm more inclined to share life, and the love of Jesus, with others and let God do the changing. But if our efforts really aren't in vain, then the love we share must play a part in God's plan to change the world.

Maybe, then, we change the world as much by loving each other as we do by trying to change it.

A good book

What do I have to offer the world? Will it be received? If it's not received, should I offer it differently?

Although I did my best to answer these questions and send them away, for a while I kept chasing after them like a bad relationship. I was never satisfied for very long with my answers. The questions were my companions whether I liked it or not.

One afternoon, I brought them with me to a San Francisco coffee house, where I entertained them once again. I remembered the characters at the beginning of the gospel of Luke: Zechariah and Elizabeth, Mary and Joseph, Simeon and Anna. Each had a part in presenting Christ to the world. Yet none sought the part. The parts, in a sense, sought them. They stepped into the parts God created for them.

I wrote in my journal, "Maybe God will create something for me to honor him." I stopped writing. I let out a silent sigh. The sentence hung in my mind as I reconnected with my surroundings. Since the last time I looked up, two or three people had sidled up to the counter. The barista was still talking about his love life, but to a different customer. A paperback had been placed on a table a few feet away from me.

A Prayer for Owen Meany by John Irving. That was title of the paperback. I was immediately taken back to a time three years prior, when I had read the novel. It's a story of destiny— of how strange incidents and routines in the life of a quirky young man prepare him for the big moment when he offers something to the world. When I read the novel, it inspired me to trust that God was preparing me, through what I was doing at the time, for what I would offer later.

When the book reappeared three years later at the coffee house, I was asking the very questions it had helped me with. What do I have to offer? Will it be received? If it's not received, should I offer it differently?

A Prayer for Owen Meany doesn't answer the questions. But I think God, in bringing the book to my attention again, wanted me to believe that the parts I have to play are not mine to create but his—and that he will create them. All I have to do is step into them and find, probably to my own surprise, that I have been prepared for them.

The owner of the paperback picked it up and took a seat near the door of the coffee house. She leafed through it, found her mark, and began reading.

As I left, I stopped next to her table. "It's a good book," I told her. "If you finish it, you might be convinced that your life has purpose." I went on my way, and she returned to the book.

I wondered about the days ahead of her.

THE WORD TAKES FLIGHT

For most of my life, I haven't owned anything, including my car, that would fetch more than five hundred dollars on the open market. One of my mottos, before getting married, was, "Never buy something your roommate might already own." I didn't know of anything that I couldn't easily—and inexpensively—replace.

Then one day, in the course of my routines, I got into my car and left my workplace. A minute later, I saw something fly by my window. At first I was startled. Then, after looking in the rear-view mirror, I was horrified. My Bible was tumbling down Middlefield Road.

Then I remembered that I had placed my Bible on the top of my car before leaving my workplace. I had planned, of course, to retrieve it after offloading other items, but I forgot. So when I drove off, the Bible slid off my car and onto the street.

My Bible, I then realized, was something I couldn't easily replace. In fact, had I lost it, I wouldn't have been able to replace it at all. It was one of a kind. It was the first Bible I had ever purchased, way back in 1974, just after coming to know Christ as a teenager. I was not concerned about the fate of my Bible for sentimental reasons, however. I was concerned because of the notes I had written in it, which were the product of countless hours of study.

The notes had value not because any particular Bible is important to me but because the word of God is important to me. The notes help me understand the word and communicate it to others. I could hardly even give away a tattered Bible with indecipherable scribbles on nearly every page, at least in this country, but to me, it's priceless.

My reaction to the possibility of losing it showed me that I valued it more than any other possession. More precisely, the possibility of losing it showed me that I valued the word of God more than any other possession. I can replace a Bible. I can't replace the word of God.

The word of God reveals God to me. It reveals the gospel: the good news that God has defeated the dark powers of the world through the death and resurrection of the Lord Jesus Christ. It leads me to worship God and follow Jesus. Apart from the word, I would be self-destructively worshiping gods of my own choosing, with money, sex, and power leading the pantheon. I wouldn't be following Jesus.

The value of the word was borne out when the people of Israel lost part of it and therefore didn't understand the dangers of worshiping other gods. When they found the Book of the Covenant (part of Exodus) in the temple, they read it to the king, who then turned to the Lord and destroyed the idols (2 Kings 22:8-23:25).

After my Bible took flight, I pulled to the side of the road and sprinted to retrieve it, beating the next wave of traffic. The binding was loose and a few of the pages were torn, and I knew that its days as a regular-use Bible were coming to an end. Soon thereafter I purchased a new Bible and spent a year transferring my notes to it.

The old Bible rests on a shelf in my study. I still pull it down occasionally when I'm working with multiple translations. It reminds me that the word of God is, in the words of David, "more precious than gold" (Psalm 19:10).

Quarters from heaven

While standing in line to place my order at a coffee house, I spotted a quarter on the floor, several paces away from me. More often than not, if I spot a coin, even a penny, I pick it up. The reason has something to do with the adage, "A penny saved is a penny earned." And a quarter—well, that's a major find.

Nonetheless, I'm not serious enough about pocketing coins to leave the line I'm in and risk looking like a money-grubber. So I decided to bide my time. I'd wait to place my order and then meander over to claim my prize.

Someone beat me to it, however. Only he didn't pocket the quarter; he dropped it in the tip jar. I was taken aback. I naturally expected the finder to do the same thing I would have done with the quarter: walk off with it.

I usually tip the baristas at least a quarter, but if I find one on the floor, I think it's mine. Perhaps God had something to say about this outlook.

Jesus offers a better adage than the old saw about a penny saved: "Freely you have received, freely give" (Matthew 10:8). Coins are the least of it. God has given me eternal life through Jesus Christ. To hold on to life is to be a miser. To give it away, to joyfully bless others with what God has given me, is to be free.

After sitting down with my coffee and books, I forgot about the quarter. An hour later I headed for the door. My path was clear—except for the quarter I almost stepped on only a few feet away from where I ogled the first one. God, it seemed, was dropping quarters from heaven—and gently, even playfully, teaching his child.

No one beat me to the quarter this time. And I knew what to do. I picked up the coin and released it into the tip jar. In my hour at the coffee house, I spotted two quarters—neither of which ended up in my pocket—and learned one valuable lesson.

Chapter 4

SEIZING THE MOMENTS (OR NOT)

The seventeenth green

In December 1995, when a relationship that was at one time heading toward marriage came to an end, I drove to the foot of a nearby hill. I climbed it and, in anger, cried out to God, "Is this what you do to people—tear them apart?"

In the following weeks, as the wounds began to heal, I came to recognize what I had already suspected: we weren't right for each other. As weeks turned into months and into years, and as I entered my forties, I wondered if I was right for anyone, and if anyone was right for me. If God tears people apart, could he be trusted with my prayers for a wife? I wasn't sure, but I worked up the courage and began asking him to bring the right woman into my life.

In the summer of 1999, I met Karen, a Stanford University Ph.D. candidate. None of the struggles that developed in the previous relationship surfaced in this one, and soon I began to hope that it would lead to marriage. My hopes were realized the following summer, when Karen and I were married.

Because I was married to a Stanford student, I was entitled to many of the students' privileges. The most prized of these, from my perspective, was access to the Stanford golf course at student rates. While growing up, I had only a mild interest in golf. My recreational time was devoted to more active pursuits. But as the years wore on, and as my knees wore down, I took to golf and found myself captivated. The venerable Stanford course has been ranked among the top one hundred in the nation. I grew up not far from it but had not played it because I had no connection that allowed me access.

In September 2000, a few days after returning from my honeymoon, I decided to exercise my new privilege. When I reached the seventeenth green, I found that it afforded a vista of the surrounding hills. The most prominent of those hills was the one I had climbed five years earlier.

As I gazed at the hill in the distance, in my mind I could hear my question: "Is this what you do to people—tear them apart?" The years seemed to carry the answer to me: "No, this is what I do to people—I bring them together." God had brought Karen and me together. We were right for each other.

At the beginning of Psalm 22, David cried out, "My God, my God, why have you forsaken me?" At first, he wasn't sure whether God could be trusted with his requests, but in the middle of the psalm, he prayed, "But you, O Lord, be not far off; / O my Strength, come quickly to help me." At the end, he wrote that the Lord had "listened to his cry for help" and had "done it"—delivered him. I felt as if I had lived Psalm 22 over the course of five years, albeit much less intensely than David, who faced enemies who wanted to kill him.

God has not always answered my cries of the heart so poetically. In fact, for the most part he hasn't answered them at all. But he's answered them often enough, and shown me his faithfulness often enough, to make me believe that I can trust him whether he answers me five minutes later, five years later, or not at all.

ANOTHER CHANCE

It could have been a nice moment, but I missed it.

My wife Karen and I were driving to church Sunday in separate cars because of our different schedules. She arrived first and parked her car. By the time I arrived, she was standing beside her car, waiting for me. When I pulled into the parking lot, she smiled at me and pointed to an open parking space next to her. But I parked in my usual spot, several spaces away from her.

"Didn't you see me?" Karen asked. Well, yes, I saw her, but I had already made up my mind where I was going to park, and I was preoccupied with my responsibilities for the morning. It wasn't until I had almost stopped my car that I realized she was inviting me to park next to her.

Two days later, as I shared coffee with a friend, I told him the story. He told me that a few days earlier, he came home from work at dinnertime with a burrito. His wife had prepared a pot of soup and offered it to him, but he ate his burrito. He regretted his actions at home, just as I regretted mine in the parking lot.

I told him, "I hope we learn to be more observant."

That afternoon Karen and I each had appointments with the same dentist. Hers was at 2:00 p.m. and mine was at 3:00 p.m. When I pulled into the parking lot, she was standing next to her car. Her appointment was over with, but she was waiting for me to arrive.

She smiled at me and pointed to an open parking spot next to her. This time, I smiled back and thought to myself, "Isn't

God good? He's giving me another chance." I parked next to her, got out of the car, and gave her a hug.

It was a nice moment, and it was impossible to miss.

The Scriptures say that God goes before us (Isaiah 45:2, Matthew 26:32). I wonder: when we get to where we're going, does God sometimes stand in front of us, smile at us, and gesture for us to come near? I think he does. We don't see the invitation with our eyes; we sense it in our hearts. But we don't respond. We have our own ideas about where we're going to park and what needs to get done.

I hope we learn to be more observant.

THE GYPSY POET

A few months after my wife and I were married, we spent a weekend at an inn overlooking the Pacific Ocean in Northern California. A little rummaging through our room turned up a journal, which had been left in the room for visitors to record their thoughts. Most of the writers, almost all of them women, occupied themselves with the joys of marital love. However, one writer, a man, wrote of love from a different angle.

He had come to the inn on three occasions: in 1985, 1990, and 2000. On his last visit, he wrote in the journal. In 1985, he came with a woman who called him the Gypsy Poet—"in love with the world and words" without not knowing he was in love with her. By 1990, the woman had married another man, and the Gypsy Poet, then thirty-three, was visiting the inn alone. He lamented that it had taken him too long to recognize love.

I saw myself in the Gypsy Poet. We were the same age. I, too, was in love with the world and words but had wondered, in my thirties and early forties, whether I had missed my appointment with love.

When the Gypsy Poet visited the inn in December 2000, he was forty-three. Again, he came alone. His final words were these: "There may remain in the world a woman of flesh and warmth, but as of tonight, my mistress is the sea. My heart remains open and my vision remains clear. Where are you tonight, this woman to steal me from my mistress so that I too might write of our love in so many years to come?"

When I visited the inn in the spring of 2001, a few months after the Gypsy Poet's last stay, I came with Karen, my new wife.

Because I saw so much of myself in the Gypsy Poet, I couldn't help thinking that I was meant to read his journal entry. It could have been me pining for a woman of flesh and warmth, but God arranged for my path to diverge from that of the Gypsy Poet. Stumbling upon the journal entry so soon after my wedding day prompted me to give thanks for Karen. The words of the Gypsy Poet reminded me—and remind me still—that Karen is God's gift to me.

I don't know why God gives the gift to some but not to others. I don't know why he gives it to some and then takes it away from them. I don't know why he makes some wait so long for it. I don't know why he gave me a woman of flesh and warmth while the Gypsy Poet cried out for one.

I do know, however, that God wants to give his greatest gift to everyone: he wants to give himself. The relationship between a man and a woman is only a faint picture of the relationship God wants with all humans, for he calls himself the bridegroom and his people the bride (Isaiah 54:5-6, Hosea 2:19-20). Even if you find a lifelong partner who inspires poetic journal entries, you still want something more than what your relationship gives. That something, the Scriptures suggest, is God.

The journal at the inn reminded me that I have a responsibility to the Gypsy poets of the world—and to everyone else, for that matter—to tell them what God has done for me (Mark 5:19). So on our last day at the inn, I added my witness to the journal. I wrote appreciatively of the Gypsy Poet, whose vulnerability allowed me to walk with him for a few steps. I wrote that at long last, I had met a woman with whom to share the years. Finally, I wrote that many years before meeting her, I met

113

the divine bridegroom, whose love transcends the years and penetrates the deepest places of the human heart. Since I met him when I was sixteen, he's been present for every heartache. I've never been alone.

A moment I didn't create

When I was six years old, I saw a bobber get pulled underwater by a trout on a pond in the Sierra Mountains. From then on, I was hooked. I love to fish. Particularly, I love to fly-fish for rising trout in mountain streams.

It was the fifth day of a six-day fishing trip with my two brothers on the Missouri River near the town of Wolf Creek, Montana. Every few years, we take a trip to the Northwest in the fall, my favorite time of year. For the first four days, the weather was beautiful. When we woke up on the fifth day, it was raining. Sometimes, clouds and rain trigger massive and long-lasting insect hatches, which cause trout to rise in large numbers throughout the day. Such was the case on the Missouri River this day. The three of us fished ourselves to exhaustion by angling for seventeen- to twenty-one-inch rainbow and brown trout for hours on end.

Near the end of the day, the storm was breaking up. The sun made its first appearance of the day and played with the clouds and mountains to create a scene of mystical contrasts. My brothers had moved to spots downstream. I was alone. I thought of my favorite scene in the film *A River Runs Through It*. At the end of the movie, Norman MacLean, now an old man, is looking back on his life while casting a fly in the fading light. He says this:

> Now, nearly all those I loved and did not understand
> in my youth are dead, even Jesse, but I still reach out
> to them. Of course, now I am too old to be much of a

fisherman, and now I usually fish the big waters alone, although some friends think I shouldn't. But when I am alone in the half-light of the canyon, all existence seems to fade to a being with my soul and memories and the sounds of the Big Blackfoot River and a four-count rhythm and the hope that a fish will rise. Eventually, all things merge into one, and a river runs through it . . . I am haunted by waters.[6]

That scene had reached into my soul many times, I think because a nostalgic streak runs through me and because dusk is my favorite time of day. On the banks of the Missouri River, alone in the half-light of the canyon, near the town of Wolf Creek, which is featured in the film, I was in some way living the scene from *A River Runs Through It*.

A few feet away from me, a large rainbow rose rhythmically. I cast my fly, and the fish took it. I set the hook, and the fish tore off downstream. As I played the fish, the storm let loose with a final cloudburst. It had only drizzled most of the day; now, for the first time, as I was fighting this mighty fish, the rain poured down. As the heavens cracked and the rain drenched me, I felt God's delight. The author of this scene, it seemed to me, was taking pleasure in it.

The cloudburst reminded me of a scene in another film that has moved me. When Andy Dufresne crawls to freedom through five hundred yards of sewage in *The Shawshank Redemption*, the rain falls and he is washed clean. The scene has inspired me in my journey toward spiritual freedom.

I reeled in the trout, a hefty nineteen-inch rainbow, and re-leased it back into the river. I climbed up the bank and took in the scene. The rain stopped, and the air was still. This thought occurred to me: "I can't create a moment like this." Days like this on a trout stream are rare. In all my years of fishing, I can remember only two other days when large trout rose consis-tently all day long.

I didn't fashion the trout. I didn't cut the river. I didn't form the clouds. I didn't cause it to rain. I didn't design the insects. I didn't coax them to hatch. I didn't convince fish to rise to them. I neither invented the sun nor brought it forth. I didn't manufacture this passion for fishing; I just found it in me. I didn't create two brothers with whom to take fishing trips and share life. I didn't paint this picture.

There I was, perched on the banks of a Montana trout stream. I was in my favorite place at my favorite time of day in my favorite season enjoying my favorite avocation and drawing inspiration from my favorite scenes in my favorite films.

In the parables of Luke 15, Jesus portrays God as a shep-herd looking for a lost sheep, as a woman searching for a lost coin, as a father searching for lost sons. We are the sheep; we are the coin; we are the sons. God is searching for us. It makes sense, then, that the one who is searching for us and created us with passions would look for us in those passions. He gave them to us in order to call out to us. He can find us in our pas-sions or in a film that moves us. He can find us in a moment that we didn't create.

On an autumn day along the banks of the Missouri River, he came and found me fishing.

FIVE LOAVES, TWO FISH, AND THREE STORIES

When I accepted an invitation to preach at evangelistic meetings in a country that is opposed to the gospel in April 2001, I was told that three hundred to four hundred people would be expected to attend each night. When I arrived, the predicted number had increased. Perhaps one thousand to two thousand would attend. When I walked out on the night of the first meeting, probably three thousand were in the audience. The second night, four thousand came. On the final night, five thousand or more people crowded into the fenced-in field.

Each night, other leaders and I were given chairs on the front platform, facing the crowd. While we sang songs and listened to announcements, I had about an hour to look out on the crowd. Each night, as I surveyed the multitude, the thought ran through my mind, "What do I have to give these people?" All I had were three stories.

The theme of the campaign was "The Risen Christ and the Church." I had prepared three messages based on the last two chapters in the gospel of John. In those chapters, Mary Magdalene, Thomas, and Peter each encounter the risen Lord Jesus. Mary has been devastated by the death of Jesus; Thomas doesn't believe that Jesus has risen from the dead; Peter is plagued by guilt for having denied his Lord. Each is bent over in pain. Jesus walks into each life, tenderly speaks to the pain, and lifts each one up with his love.

I believe in the power of God's love. Therefore, I believe in the power of the biblical story and the numerous smaller stories contained within it. It's a love story made up of many love stories. I have also come to believe that telling these stories is central to my vocation.

When five thousand hungry people gathered around Jesus, his disciples had five loaves and two fish. Jesus blessed the food and kept giving it to the disciples, who kept giving it to the multitude. Luke writes, "They all ate and were satisfied" (Luke 9:10-17).

All the disciples had were five loaves and two fish. All I had were three stories.

They are God's stories, and if they are God's stories, they are powerful. So I stood up each night and told the stories. I told them about Jesus, the bread of life, whose love satisfies the hunger in the human heart. What did the people come for, and why did they keep coming? They were hungry. As one of the organizers put it, "I sense a strong hunger for the love of Christ here tonight."

The first night, when we extended an invitation to the crowd at the conclusion of the meeting, more than one hundred people came forward and said they wanted to begin following Jesus. The second night, even more came forward. The third night, we couldn't ask them to come forward, because there was no room in the front; the entire field was filled with people. Instead, we asked them to stand. One thousand, maybe two thousand or three thousand, rose to partake of the bread of life.

They all ate and were satisfied.

New perspective

I'd been meeting weekly with Joe for a year with hopes of leading him to Christ. But he wasn't responding. Finally, I pushed for a decision. I told him to follow Jesus; he told me to back off.

I wondered if I was wasting my time. If my purpose for our meetings—leading him to Christ—was failing, then why bother? Perhaps it was time to bring our meetings to an end. Joe, however, wanted to continue meeting.

In order for me to continue meeting with Joe, I would need a new perspective. Joe enjoyed our meetings. I enjoyed them also. Why, then, was I frustrated? Because I conceived of Joe as a project. No matter how much I enjoyed our meetings, I considered them a failure unless they resulted in a decision for Christ.

I repented. I decided to stop thinking of Joe as a project and start thinking of him as a person. I decided to stop pushing him and to simply let him decide in his own time. And I decided to continue meeting with him.

We studied the Scriptures together and discussed spirituality. For me, the pressure was off. No longer laboring under the burden of leading Joe to Christ, I simply enjoyed him.

Another year went by. Then one morning, we met for coffee at our usual spot.

"I'm ready," he said.

"Ready for what?"

"To be baptized."

How about that.

I suggested that he write a prayer. We walked outside to a nearby park, where Joe read his prayer. That day, he began to follow Jesus.

We celebrated a few weeks later. Joe, his family, and a few friends shared a meal. Then we drove to the coast, where Joe and I waded into the Pacific Ocean. I eased him under the waves. When I brought him up, he said it was cold. But he felt good. I felt good, too.

Jesus said, "No one can come to me unless the Father who sent me draws him" (John 6:44). I know a man from another country who was dragged before the local magistrate and accused of converting people to Christ. He answered, "I can't convert anyone. Only God can convert someone. Could I convert you?" The official let him go. I can't convert anyone; only God can. If this is so, I must cooperate with what God is doing instead of pushing my own agenda.

I helped Joe learn to follow Jesus, but only after I stopped pushing him. Joe helped me learn that a man is person, not a project.

OUT OF A JOB

In the spring of 1993, I was asked to be the interim director of a biblical studies center at a church in Idaho. I went overseas that summer, but I also prepared for my new job, which would begin in the fall. When I returned, the church had already found a permanent director. I was out of a job before I had even started it.

I was offered a job and spent two months preparing for it; then the offer was rescinded. If God had anything to do with this, what, I wondered, was it?

A year later, I accepted a permanent job as a pastor at the church in California where I continue to serve to this day. It had a similar study center, but I would not be responsible for it. I was busy with my work, and others were better positioned to lead the program. Then, in the spring of 2001, the church needed a new director for the program. The elders offered me the ministry, and I accepted.

In perusing files covering the thirty-year history of the church's training program, I came upon the names of several men who had graduated from the program and had been instrumental in training me. I think the Lord wanted me to know that he was entrusting to me a program that had, in a roundabout way, trained me.

So, what was God doing in the summer of 1993? I was studying to lead a program on an interim basis, but I couldn't help dreaming about what I would do on a long-term basis. I was studying—and I was dreaming. In the following years, I continued to study, in connection with my pastoral work, and to dream about leading a training program. In 1993, I was preparing for a non-existent job, but God was preparing me, and inspiring me, for a job he would give me eight years later. I guess I needed eight years of preparation, not just one summer.

Moses had a dream. He wanted to liberate his people from Egypt. But they rejected his leadership, so he fled to the wilderness, where he wasted away as a shepherd, for all he could tell. Forty years later, God gave Moses the job, sending him back to Egypt as a liberator. The wilderness years did their work: Moses learned to lead a flock. Now the flock was a nation, not a herd, but he was ready. God shaped his man by denying him the job he would give him forty years later (Exodus 2-3, Acts 7:20-29).

What was God doing some 3,400 years ago? He was shaping Moses. What was he doing in the summer of 1993? He was shaping me. What's he doing now? He's shaping me still.

NO AGENDA

What's it like to wake up without an agenda? For a long time, I didn't know, because I couldn't remember waking up without one. Even my vacations, most of which were oriented around fly-fishing, included agendas. When I fish, I'm on a mission to catch trout. When I wake up on fishing trips, I'm fixated on trout.

When I took a sabbatical with no agenda other than to poke around Italy and Spain for two months with my wife, I didn't know what to expect. Our plan was to find places and stay for five to seven days before moving on. We went on no more than one major outing a day, usually in the afternoon, to a museum or another site of interest. My mornings mostly consisted of reading, journaling, and walking. We only had to ponder the nature of the outing and what city to visit next—nothing urgent.

I made no phone calls and sent no e-mails, nor did I receive any. Work seemed like part of another life.

I didn't know what this would do for me. In Europe, feelings and memories rose repeatedly and forcefully from my subconscious like steam from a geyser. At home, the issues of the moment usually keep feelings and memories from surfacing for long. In Europe, dreams from the previous night lingered with me throughout the day. At home, if I wake up with a dream in my head, I quickly dismiss it and get on with my day.

In Europe, I decided to go with it. I let my feelings, memories, and dreams have their way with me. I wanted to see where they would take me.

Most mornings, I wrote in a journal. I recorded my impressions and tried to understand them. I wanted to know what they were telling me about myself and about my conception of God. As I wrote, feelings, memories, and dreams set off a chain reaction in my mind. Trying to understand one impression only triggered a second impression, which in turn triggered a third impression, which . . . well, even without an agenda, I had to stop writing eventually. At best I was only able to assign partial meaning to my impressions. Complete understanding eluded me. For the most part, my impressions ran away from me, and I could not capture them.

I looked inside and saw a whirlpool of passions. I spent two months attempting to know myself and came to the conclusion that I don't know myself very well. I feel, I remember, and I dream, but I don't know what it all means. I don't know how everything contributes to my motives or even what, in the end, motivates me. I know God, but I'm not all that sure sometimes what I really think about him. I can be moved to tears by thoughts of him one moment and disregard him the next.

I wonder if this gets in the way of following Jesus. Am I not doing what God wants me to do because I don't even know what's in my heart? Do I conceive of God in such a way that I'm disinclined to obey him? Which passions should I heed and which should I shun?

David knew that he didn't know himself, so he prayed: "Search me, O God, and know my heart; / test me and know my anxious thoughts. / See if there is any offensive way in me, / and lead me in the way everlasting" (Psalm 139:23-24).

I may not know myself well, but God knows me fully (1 Corinthians 13:12). Because I don't know myself, I *need* God to know me. If I invite him to search my heart, I can hope he'll reveal to me what I need to know and lead me in the way of Jesus.

Moment of Decision

Twice I have visited the Academia museum in Florence to see Michelangelo's David. The first time, I spent an hour with the sculpture. The second time, I spent three hours. On both occasions, I felt as if someone were speaking to me: David, Michelangelo, maybe God.

I know little about art, but I like a good story. The story behind the David, as depicted in Irving Stone's *The Agony and the Ecstasy*, is a great one. Great art and a great story make a powerful combination.

Michelangelo planned to shape David out of a two-thousand-pound, seventeen-foot column of marble. It was a daunting task, not least because the column was gouged in the center. Michelangelo, like sculptors before him, at first intended to capture David after his victory over Goliath. This artist, though, couldn't resonate with David's experience of victory and concluded that David before he entered the fray was a more worthy subject. He decided to depict David at the moment he decided to take on Goliath.

Stone writes: "Was not the decision more important than the act itself, since character was more critical than action? For him, then, it was David's decision that made him a giant, not his killing of Goliath. He had been floundering because he had imprisoned himself and David at the wrong moment in time."

On both visits to the Academia, I was taken by David's face. It reflects, as Stone writes, "fear, hesitation, repugnance, doubt." In Michelangelo's mind, David loved the pastoral life and was reluctant to leave it for the courts of kings. If he defeated Goliath, as he expected to, his life would never be the same. Michelangelo came to conceive of David as representing every man. Not everyone conquers Goliath, but everyone faces decisions whether to "strike for freedom," in Stone's words.

Backtracking in David's life to the moment of decision opened up new vistas for Michelangelo. Stone again: "The limitations of the block began to appear as assets, forcing his mind into a simplicity of design that might never have occurred to him had it been whole and perfect."[7]

When I scrutinized David's face, I thought, "That's me." I crave the contemplative life: reading, writing, reflecting. But something within me also wants to enter the fray and strike for freedom. Perhaps like Everyman, I live with a tension between the contemplative life and the active life. David, though, must have learned to live with it: he was Israel's greatest leader *and* its greatest poet.

When I took in the David as a whole, I marveled that it was crafted out of a flawed column of marble. I'm better suited, by temperament and personality, for the contemplative life. As a leader, I'm limited. Ah, but maybe I need to think of leadership differently. A colleague once told me, "Your problem is you want all the gifts." Perhaps, like Michelangelo's column of marble, my limitations are assets, if they force me to let God work through me just as I am instead of as I'd like to be. The apostle Paul learned to value his weaknesses because they taught him to depend on the power of Christ (2 Corinthians 12:7-10).

I learned, both from Michelangelo and from Irving Stone, to appreciate the tension between my contemplative and active impulses and that limitations can be assets. If I visit the Academia again, I might spend a day there.

THE INNKEEPER

As my wife and I strolled along a seaside walkway in the village of Monterosso, on the Italian Riviera, I was keeping an eye out for familiar sites. During a vacation thirteen years earlier, I had visited the village with a friend. One person we had met, an innkeeper, was particularly memorable.

When I had visited Monterosso the first time, Mark and I ambled into Andrea Poggi's hotel, looking for a place to stay. I trotted out about the only Italian words I knew to ask about a night's lodging. The innkeeper let me stumble all the way to the end of my awkward inquiry before proclaiming, "Señor, you speak perfect Italian." The fact of the matter was that Andrea Poggi spoke perfect English. Before answering my question about lodging, he said, "Have some wine." He escorted Mark and me to a corner and poured us each a glass of the family vintage. He regaled us with stories of his village and his family, which could trace its roots in Monterosso to the fifteenth century. Of course we decided to stay.

We ate dinner at his restaurant as well. Andrea enlivened our meal with friendly interjections. When I asked him about an item on the menu, he said, "They're mussels. They make you sexy." All in all, Andrea Poggi made our stay in Monterosso a delightful one.

When I returned thirteen years later, I wondered whether Andrea was still running his hotel. I examined the buildings along the walkway, trying to remember which was his. I looked through the window of one of the buildings and saw a man at the counter conversing with a pair of patrons. He looked older, to be sure, but it was Andrea Poggi. I turned to my wife and pronounced, "It's the same guy!"

Karen and I ambled into Andrea's hotel. Speaking in English this time, I said, "Señor Poggi, thirteen years ago I stayed at your hotel and ate dinner at your restaurant. You told me that if I ate your mussels, they would make me sexy. Well, I ate your mussels, and in order to prove to you that they have made me sexy, I return to you with a wife."

Do you know what he said?

"Have some wine."

He escorted Karen and me to the corner and poured us each a glass of wine—the family vintage, of course. We shared some stories for a few minutes; then he had to return to work. Karen and I bade him farewell and resumed our seaside stroll.

I can hardly make it through a day, it seems, without being reminded of a previous day. The same was true for Jacob, who spent twenty years facing into his past, bracketed by two encounters with God (Genesis 28:10-22, 32:1-32). The second encounter echoed the first encounter. Each featured the same locale, the presence of angels, the naming of a place, and the sun as a backdrop.

The second encounter was not a rerun, however, for it also featured differences. When Jacob met God the second time, he was returning to the Promised Land, not leaving it; he was facing into his past, not running from it; he was traveling with a large family instead of by himself; the sun was rising, not setting.

The striking combination of similarities and dissimilarities makes a point: Jacob had become a new man. The second encounter let Jacob know that God had been faithful to him, and it strengthened him to assume his destiny as the father of a nation.

When one scene in life echoes a previous scene, perhaps God is showing us how far he's taken us, and that he's with us still. When I came to Monterosso the second time, much had changed. I had changed. I came as a newly married man. Unlike Jacob, I was not yet a father—but I was about to be. The words of an Italian innkeeper reminded me that the Lord had been faithful, and they strengthened me for the future.

OUT AT THE PLATE

One morning, I woke up with a vivid memory of something that had happened almost twenty years earlier. Nothing in particular triggered the memory. I hadn't thought of it in many years. I just woke up with it.

I was the shortstop on a softball team. We had a one-run lead in the bottom of the last inning. The other team's best hitter was up. He hit a screaming line drive to left-center field. It looked as if it would be a home run. Our left fielder ran down the ball. I positioned myself for the cutoff, and he threw a perfect strike to me. As I turned around to make the throw to home, I saw the runner rounding third and realized that we had a chance to get him if my throw was good. My throw was good. The catcher applied the tag, the runner was out, and we won the game.

I lingered with the memory for several moments and found that I was fond of it. I enjoyed the memory so much because people had come together for a common purpose and everyone had done his part. For one beautiful, magical, poetic moment, everything had come together.

I think God excavated that memory to show me my heart for the church. I want us to come together to worship the Lord and carry the love of Christ to the world. I want everyone to have a part. I want everything to come together in a poetic movement of the Spirit of God.

Who are we? What stirs our hearts? What should we do with our lives? The answers may be rattling around in our collection of memories. Who was Jesus? What stirred his heart? What did he do with his life? He was the Son of God, sent by God to rescue the world from sin and death by dying on a cross.

When Jesus was dying, the passersby taunted him, saying, "Come down from the cross, if you are the Son of God." Jesus had heard such words before. When he was just starting out, he was fasting in the wilderness when the devil told him, "If you are the Son of God, tell these stones to become bread." He knew, however, that the Son of God must not submit to the enemy of God.

In the voices of the passersby, Jesus heard the hiss of the serpent. He could have called on twelve legions of angels and come down from the cross just as easily as he could have eaten the devil's bread. Inadvertently, the passersby reminded Jesus who he was and of his encounter with the devil. He had resisted the devil in the wilderness. He knew he must defeat him on the cross. Yes, he was the Son of God. No, he would not come down from the cross (Matthew 4:3, 26:53, 27:40).

Every once in a while, a memory breaks loose, and we feel today what we felt in earlier days. Are we all that different today, if what touched us then touches us now? If not, then maybe God is the one who kicks loose a memory to show us who we are, what stirs our hearts, and what he wants us to do.

LIKE EATING SPINACH

I set for myself an agenda of meditating on one passage of Scripture over the course of two days. In all, I spent ten hours with Philippians 2:5-11. I didn't study the text. Instead, I sat with it—dwelling on it and praying through it.

I'm not very good at this sort of thing, and I can't say that I enjoy it very much. I thrive on studying the Scriptures; meditating on them puts me to sleep. I get bored and distracted easily. To be honest, I expected more of the same when I chose to meditate on the Philippians passage. I did it more out of discipline than anything else. For me, meditating on Scripture is like eating spinach: I may not like it, but it's supposed to be good for me.

In Philippians 2:5-11, Paul tells the story of Christ in a few lines of poetry. The passage is a story and a poem about Jesus. I love stories, I love poems, and I love Jesus. So if I'm going to pick a passage to keep me company for ten hours, this seemed to be a good one. Paul writes that Christ, though he was "in very nature God," did not use the status, power, and privileges of deity to his own advantage. Instead, he "made himself nothing" by becoming a human servant with no rights, finally suffering for the sins of the world.

I'm sorry to report that I spent much of the ten hours fighting sleep. I tried to bring my wandering mind back to the passage, but most of the time it headed off in a different direction.

At one point, however, I was able to stay with the passage for about an hour. Paul introduces the story with these words: "Your attitude should be the same as that of Christ Jesus." The story of Christ was beckoning me to conceive of myself as a servant with no rights. As I meditated on the passage, I realized that my attitude bore little resemblance to that of Christ. I am fiercely attached to status, power, and privileges. I like my rights. I want more of them.

My essential predicament, I concluded, is that I want to be God. I want the status, power, and privileges that come with deity. Earlier, when meditating on the passage, I was bored. Now I was horrified.

What does one do with such a realization? My attachment to status, power, and privileges was so strong that I felt unable simply to let go of them. I confessed my desire to be God to the true God and prayed that he would deliver me. Today, some years later, I don't feel delivered. I'm more aware of my predicament, but I haven't moved beyond it.

Yet, awareness has its benefits. First, if Philippians 2:5-11 is supposed to humble me, it's done its work. The realization that I'm attached to rights, when I know I'm not supposed to be, humbles me. Second, my realization that I'm attached to rights doesn't mean I have to act based on that attachment. In fact, awareness of sinful proclivities enables me to consciously oppose them instead of unknowingly submitting to them. Third, my desire to be God makes me thankful that I'm not God, for I know I wouldn't have done with deity what Christ Jesus did with it. I would seek my own benefit, but he made himself nothing and suffered for my sins.

For ten hours, as I meditated on the story of Christ, I was mostly bored. For one hour, I was attentive. Were the other nine hours a waste of time? I think not.

The psalmist says the one who meditates on the Scriptures is "like a tree planted by streams of water, which yields its fruit in season and whose leaf does not wither" (Psalm 1:3). The Holy Spirit works at the deepest levels of our beings in ways that transcend awareness. I take it, then, that I sank my roots deeper into the story of Christ, and that all ten hours will contribute to spiritual stability and spiritual fruitfulness.

THE OTHER SIDE OF THE BOAT

I've made it a practice to repeatedly read through the Bible in three years' time. When I finish, I start over again. If something from the text opens my heart, it's usually when I'm studying it, not reading it. I study for depth; I read for breadth. On occasion, however, in the course of simply reading the text, something from it strikes me just so, and I sense that God is telling me something.

On one particular day, I opened to John 21, which was next on my reading schedule.

The apostle John reports that Peter and other disciples of Jesus fished all night but caught nothing. In the morning, Jesus called out to them from the shore and told them to throw their net on the other side of the boat. They took his advice and couldn't haul in the net because of the large number of fish that filled it.

Jesus earlier told Peter and the other disciples, "I am the vine; you are the branches. If a man remains in me and I in him, he will bear much fruit; apart from me you can do nothing" (John 15:7). On his own, Peter caught "nothing." With Jesus calling the shots, Peter caught a miracle.

I've translated John 21 from Greek, the language of the New Testament, to English. I've studied it thoroughly. I've taught on it, both at home and abroad. The passage has instructed me, but this time, it pried open my heart.

I can easily tie myself into knots trying to figure out what to do. I often wonder if I should employ some new approach that would be more effective. Before embarking in a new direction,

I usually analyze it from every side. I was struck, however, by the simplicity and effectiveness of the change that Peter made. All he did was throw the net on the other side of the boat. One minute he had no fish; the next minute he had 153.

I suppose change is not as complicated as I've made it out to be. Instead of analyzing change, perhaps I should simply be ready to make it when Jesus tells me to.

Ah, but if he wants me to throw my net on the other side of the boat, will he call out to me from the shore, and will I be able to hear him? Well, I think I heard him when I was reading John 21. I don't think he was telling me to make a change; I think he was telling me to be ready to make a change.

Since then, I've made some changes. I don't know if I've heard Jesus instructing me to make them or not, but since reading John 21, they've been easier to make. Near as I can tell, they haven't resulted in dramatic increases in effectiveness, but they've been for the better. I wouldn't be surprised, though, if in the future a simple change, like throwing my net on the other side of the boat, produces shocking results.

In any event, I'll keep reading the Scriptures. I don't expect that to change.

Chapter 5

FAMILY MAN

ULTRASOUND VISION

Ultrasound images of my first daughter inside my wife's womb aroused in me what I can only presume to be fatherly instincts. I saw her stretch out her little legs and put her little thumb in her mouth. She looked vulnerable to me, and I wondered if she was all right in there. I wanted to help her.

Before my daughter was born, some friends told me that she would wrap me around her little finger. I told them, "She's already done it." She wrapped me around her little finger when I saw her stretch out her little legs and put her little thumb in her mouth.

Jesus told a story that compared God to a farmer who planted a vineyard (Luke 20:9-16). God's people are like tenants who rented the vineyard. The prophets are like servants of the farmer. The farmer sent a servant to collect some fruit from the vineyard, but the tenants beat him. Not deterred, the father sent another servant, but they beat him as well. Surely, we think, the farmer won't send any more servants, but he sends a third, who is also beaten.

Finally, the farmer says, "What shall I do? I will send my son, whom I love; perhaps they will respect him." And we think,

"Are you crazy? You've seen what they've done to your servants; what do you think they'll do to your son?" When the tenants see the son, they kill him and throw him out of the vineyard. The son, of course, represents God's Son. We wanted this world for ourselves. We sent God's Son packing.

As I looked at my daughter, ten inches in length and one pound in weight, I thought of the Father, and I thought of the Son. This, I thought, is how God sent his Son into the world, as a helpless child clinging to life inside his mother's womb. And I thought to myself, "Are you crazy? Are you crazy for sending your Son into this vineyard in this way? Don't you know what they'll do to him?"

This is what God is like: a crazy farmer. He opens up his heart so that we will give him something of our hearts. We reject him and abuse him, and he opens his heart wider and wider until he lets go of the one he values most, his Son, hoping against hope that we will see into his heart.

Through the window of modern technology, I not only saw my daughter, I also saw what God wants me to see most: his heart.

What's in a Name?

When someone asked me whether the name my wife and I would choose for our first child was important, I answered, "I don't know." But I did know this: I wanted to involve God in the process.

When Zechariah and Elizabeth had a son, they were expected to give him a family name. But an angel told Zechariah to name the boy John, even though none of couple's relatives was named John. The name was connected to the boy's destiny. He is known to us today as John the Baptist (Luke 1:11-17, 59-63).

A name might be important. Perhaps God had a name in mind for our child. If so, perhaps he would make it known to us. So Karen and I began to pray.

I started out wanting a name that was three or more syllables and which ended in a vowel, which, I figured, would go well with a one-syllable last name that begins with a consonant (Grant). Karen and I began suggesting names to each other. Our plan was to settle on a name for a while and see how it resonated with us. One of the first names that Karen suggested was Christina. It didn't immediately sit well with me, so I eliminated it. My first suggestion met with Karen's approval, but in time we discovered that it was a trendy name, so we dismissed it. We settled on another name, this one with four syllables, but soon we began to feel more comfortable with a three-syllable name, so that one, too, fell by the wayside.

About a month before our daughter was born, the name Christina resurfaced in my mind. When it did, it sounded right to me. I don't know what caused the name to resurface or why I liked it the second time. Karen was delighted, for she had been fond of the name ever since she was a little girl. So, how would the name Christina play out?

Two weeks before the due date, we visited an Italian restaurant in San Francisco. I had dined there perhaps a dozen times and had befriended the owner, an immigrant who enjoyed playing the over-the-top Italian restaurateur for his patrons. When Franchino saw me this time with my pregnant wife, he was particularly excited.

"We're having a girl," I told him.

"I'll tell you what you should name her," he said. "Just one minute."

He turned away for a moment, searching for—or pretending to search for—a name.

"Christina!" he said. "It is a good Italian name."

Not long after we were married, Karen and I had spent five weeks in Italy, our favorite country. When the restaurateur said "Christina," we knew our search was over.

A name that a little girl takes a liking to, a name that years later her husband initially dismisses as a name for their first child but mysteriously embraces the second time around, a name that is suggested out of the blue by a restaurant owner—that's the name we chose for our daughter. Or perhaps God, having plans for the name beyond our knowing, helped us choose it.

God in our arms

When my first daughter emerged from my wife's womb, the doctor held her up for me to see. A team of nurses carried her to a table in the delivery room, cleaned her, and wrapped her in a towel. Then they handed her to me, and I took her in my arms.

In the film *Paint Your Wagon*, a woman and her baby come to a mining outpost composed entirely of men. As word of the woman's arrival spreads, the men flock to the outskirts of town to get a look at her. By all appearances, the woman should be concerned for her safety. One of the men, a burly miner, approaches the woman and says, "Ma'am, I'll give you fifty dollars if you'll let me hold the baby." He gives the woman the money and takes the baby in his enormous arms, cradling her against his bare chest.[8]

A man named Simeon who lived in Jerusalem in the first century was waiting for the salvation of his people. God revealed to him that he would live to see the answer: the Messiah. One day, the Holy Spirit moved him to approach a man and a woman who had brought their baby into the temple courts. This baby, he discerned, was the one.

Indeed, as God had promised, Simeon lived to see the Messiah. What did he do then? Luke tells us that Simeon "took him in his arms." After embracing the baby, Simeon told God that he was ready to die (Luke 2:21-35).

What is it about holding a baby that can turn even the most hardened of us into jelly? Simple vulnerability.

It is a great paradox that God displays his power in weakness: the weakness of a baby lying in a manger, the weakness of a man hanging on a cross. God didn't have to become a baby. The man on the cross could have summoned twelve legions of angels. It takes strength to become weak. The story of Jesus is so powerful because it's a story of vulnerability. It draws us in. We want to believe it. Perhaps, even, we want to be part of it.

The story of Simeon is a story for us. It's a story about us. Simeon is not one of the Bible's towering figures. He's an ordinary man who passes from the pages of the Scriptures as quickly as he arrives. He's a man like us. We become part of the story when we take his part—the part written for us as well as for him.

Like Simeon, we're waiting for the answer. The Holy Spirit moves us toward Jesus. In the story of Simeon, God makes himself vulnerable and says, "Take me in your arms."

Ten minutes of terror

I waited a long time for Christina, my first child. I was forty-five when she was born. When she was a few months old, she fell ill with a fever. I gave her a cool bath, but as I was changing her diaper, her eyes rolled back into her head. "Is this normal?" I wondered. Then her little body stiffened and trembled.

She was having a seizure. Panic-stricken, I handed her to my wife and called 911. Karen cradled Christina and kept speaking her name to her. By the time the paramedics arrived, some ten minutes later, the seizure had passed.

The paramedics told us that Christina had suffered a febrile seizure, which afflicts some one in twenty-five infants. It's somewhat normal. The pediatrician later told us not to worry if it happened again and that there was no need to call medical personnel.

A seizure? Normal? I suppose parents learn something new every day, but that's something I wish I had known before my daughter started shaking. It would have saved me ten minutes of terror. If she was dying, I would have done anything to keep her alive. I would have gladly given my life for hers. Beyond picking up the phone, there was nothing I could do. And she was my only child.

God had a Son—only one. What was it like for the Father as his Son was dying on the cross? The Son cried out, "My God, my God, why have you forsaken me?" Where was the Father when his Son needed him? Unfathomably, he held himself back. But he made his feelings known.

The Son had told Simon Peter and his other followers to take up crosses and follow him. Simon Peter, though, disowned the Son, so the Father sent another Simon, Simon of Cyrene, to carry the Son's cross. After moving Simon of Cyrene onto the stage, the Father changed the backdrop: he darkened creation from noon to 3:00 p.m. to mourn for his Son. The Father's heart was being ripped open, so he tore the veil of the temple from top to bottom. He shook the land, trembling with grief. When the Son was just starting out, the Father had said, "This is my Son, whom I love; with him I am well pleased." After his Son had breathed his last, the Father sent some soldiers to proclaim, "Surely he was the Son of God." Although the Father restrained himself, he found a way to say, "That's my Son!" (Matthew 3:17, 16:24, 27:27-54).

My ten minutes of terror gave me a window into the Father's love for his Son. I don't presume to understand it, but I think I understand it better.

This, however, I don't understand: whereas I would have done anything to rescue my daughter, the Father did nothing to rescue his Son. I did what I could, which wasn't much: I made a phone call. The Father, on the other hand, could have moved heaven and earth and he didn't do it.

Why? It has to do with his love for us. The Son came into to the world to rescue us from the dark powers of sin and death. As he hung on the cross, some mockers said, "Let God rescue him now if he wants him, for he said, 'I am the Son of God'" (Matthew 27:43). God didn't rescue his Son because he wanted us. To rescue us, he had to watch the dark powers do their worst to his Son.

I don't understand it.

THE TEARS OF A TWO-YEAR-OLD

I was reading the story of Adam and Eve from a children's Bible to my daughter Christina, who was two years old. She was a particularly sensitive little girl. Even pictures of sleeping teddy bears disturbed her.

When we came to the page that pictured Adam and Eve after they had disobeyed God, Christina asked me, "Why are they sad?"

"They made a mistake," I said.

Christina began sobbing uncontrollably. At first, her response startled me. Then I realized that it was utterly appropriate.

Our world downplays sin, even jokes about it. If it takes sin seriously at all, it defines it as isolated acts of misguided behavior. But where does such behavior come from? It comes from the human heart, and the prophet Jeremiah says, "The heart is deceitful above all things and beyond cure" (Jeremiah 17:9).

Why is the human heart thus? We were made to worship God and serve him in his creation, but we have turned our backs on him. We're creatures of worship, though, so we must worship something. Therefore, we've chosen to worship other gods that are more to our liking, such as money, sex, and power. The sin we're guilty of, the sin that gives birth to all the sins, is high treason against our sovereign creator (Romans 1:18-32, 3:10-18). We've become the rebel rulers of our own lives. Our hearts are all messed up.

Count me among those who downplay sin. Yes, I've joked about it, too. I don't want to acknowledge it in myself because to do so means to acknowledge that there's something wrong with me. If there's something wrong with me, then I need help, and I'd rather not accept any help, thank you. To accept help means I'm not as in charge of my life as I'd like to be, and—well, I guess I'm back to the essence of sin: I'd rather run my life than submit to God. My heart is all messed up.

Yes, I need help. There's only one thing that can help with sin, and that's to be forgiven for it. And the only one who can forgive me for sin is the one I've sinned against: God. He can help, but will he? The apostle Paul says he's already done it: "But God demonstrates his own love for us in this: While we were still sinners, Christ died for us" (Romans 5:8). God sent his Son in order to forgive me.

To be forgiven: that's the help I need. That's the help God has given me. In order to appreciate it and the one who gives it, I need to be reminded of my otherwise desperate condition.

The tears of a two-year-old did the job. For a few moments, when Christina wept over the story of Adam and Eve, I wanted to weep with her.

THE NEW WAY

I've driven every imaginable route to Inverness, though not by design. I visit the Northern California town at least once a year for a personal retreat between Christmas and New Year's. The unpredictable weather that time of year makes traveling problematic. I've often found myself driving in a downpour.

My preferred route is to cross over to the coast near Sausalito and drive north on Highway 1. Sometimes, however, rains have washed out the route and I've had to find different ways to get to Inverness. On one such occasion, I made it almost all the way to Highway 1 but had to backtrack to U.S. 101, work my way north, and take another road to the coast. It wouldn't be as scenic as the coastal route, I figured, but I'd get there.

I was wrong. Oh, I got there, but the inland route this day—maybe this day more than any other day—was breathtaking. The heavy rains created rivulets, cascades, and even waterfalls along the hills that lined the road. Because of the wet conditions on the winding road, I took a leisurely pace, which enabled me to enjoy nature's surprise. Frustrated at first, I was thankful in the end.

I have my preferred routes: my routine, my way of doing things. I prefer them because they've satisfied me. Nothing is wrong with my ways unless I get stuck in them and become unable to perceive or take a new way that God creates for me.

In exile, Israel got into a routine. God told his people, "See, I am doing a new thing! / Now it springs up; do you not perceive it? / I am making a way in the desert and streams in the wasteland" (Isaiah 43:19). Israel needed to be aware that God would create a way for her to return to the Promised Land. She needed to be perceptive, not complacent.

Sometimes, God makes me perceptive. When I was driving to Inverness, I perceived that my way was blocked. I couldn't go any farther, so I had to look for another way. It happens all the time: God blocks my way and creates a new way. At first, I'm usually frustrated. Then, if I'm courageous to take the new way, I'm thankful.

The old way is predictable. I can count on it to satisfy me. The new way, however, is fraught with unknowns. I don't know whether it will satisfy me, bore me, or kill me. With the old way, I'm more likely to trust myself. With the new way, I'm more likely to trust God. For me, taking the new way creates trust in the one who created the new way. What I need, more than anything, is to trust God.

The new way, if God has created it, goes through his heart. What did I see as I took the new road to Inverness? God made streams not in the wasteland, as in Isaiah's vision, but on the hillsides, and they delighted my eyes. God is faithful, I thought. God is beautiful, I also thought. What did I see? I saw his faithful, beautiful heart.

I'll try to be perceptive, to watch for the new way, and courageous, to take the new way, because I want to see God's heart.

Spiritual direction

The conversation was unsettling. I had come to the retreat house for my annual pilgrimage, and I had met another person who was also on a retreat. When I shared with her some of my concerns as a pastor, she flooded me with a torrent of potential solutions. I come to this place once a year to breathe fresh spiritual air, but I was drowning in this conversation. I couldn't connect with any of her solutions. They may have worked for someone else, but none of them was right for me. I would have been like David, who unsuccessfully tried to fit into Saul's armor (1 Samuel 17:38-39).

Removed from the stresses of daily life, I had always slept well at the retreat house. But now my mind was spinning, and I lay awake most of the night. Come morning, a comment from my new friend was still with me. It didn't concern one of her solutions; it simply concerned her presence at the retreat house. She had told me was there to see her spiritual director, Father Tom.

I had known Father Tom as parish priest since I began coming to the retreat house eight years earlier. But I was unaware that he was also a spiritual director. Earlier in the year, I had begun thinking about seeking a spiritual director, but I wasn't motivated enough to do anything about it. Before leaving the retreat house, however, I considered asking Father Tom about spiritual direction. In the end, I decided against it, mostly because I was reticent to entertain something new and mysterious. Maybe I'd call him later after mulling it over, I reasoned.

I went for one final walk around the grounds, but a fallen tree blocked my path. I backtracked and headed for my car.

I looked up, and Father Tom was walking toward me, on his way to the retreat house. He was unavoidable.

So I asked him about spiritual direction. He said he helps people see how the Holy Spirit is moving them toward God. His description delighted me. "I'm an Episcopalian priest who's strongly influenced by the Eastern Orthodox Church," he told me. "I do spiritual direction for sixteen people, eleven of whom are evangelical pastors."

I wondered how the pastors found him. He's outside their spiritual tradition, and he doesn't advertise. I'd been visiting his retreat house for eight years without knowing he was a spiritual director. Apparently, God leads pastors to this man. To lead me, he used an unsettling conversation and he uprooted a tree.

I think that if I'm to take a new path, I must motivate myself to strike out on my own. But oftentimes, God makes the new path unavoidable. It's almost as if I don't have a choice in the matter. An angel of the Lord, quite literally, blocked Balaam's path and redirected him (Numbers 22:22-35).

All told, I met with Father Tom for five years, once every three months, before our paths diverged. My pastoral concerns did not dissipate, but they became less intense. More importantly, Father Tom helped me see how the Holy Spirit was moving me, in the midst of my concerns, toward God.

Seek and You Will Find

"My name is Shawn," said the message on my answering machine. "I met you in Basalt, Colorado, at a coffee shop, and you gave me your card."

As the message continued, I eventually, though vaguely, remembered talking to someone when I was vacationing in Colorado three years earlier. After fishing for trout one morning, I had been resting and reading in a coffee house. That's when I had met Shawn. We couldn't have talked for more than ten minutes.

When I'm speaking with people who aren't yet followers of Jesus, I'll often tell them this: "If you seek Jesus, you'll find Jesus." It's nothing original. Jesus said, "Ask and it will be given to you; seek and you will find; knock and the door will be opened to you" (Matthew 7:7). God told Israel, "You will seek me and find me when you seek me with all your heart" (Jeremiah 29:13).

Shawn's message continued: "I was just calling because I have your card and wanted to tell you thank you. You told me to 'keep looking toward Jesus' and that 'if you seek him, you'll find him.' And as a result of that, I kept going in that direction, and I just wanted to thank you for that."

I've suggested this to dozens of people. Mostly, I never see or hear from them again. I tend to assume that they have neither sought nor found Jesus, at least not at my behest.

Now I wonder. Perhaps others have also followed my advice and found Jesus. Perhaps only Shawn had the wherewithal to make a phone call. After all, I don't hand my card out to everyone.

Frankly, I don't remember telling Shawn to seek Jesus, nor do I remember giving him my card. Nothing in our interaction made me believe that something significant was transpiring. In the morning, I had gone fishing. In the afternoon, I went fishing. I remember the trout streams well, but I barely remember Shawn.

A few days after receiving Shawn's message, some friends and I spoke with a stranger about Jesus. Although he kept asking questions, he seemed uninterested in our answers. By the end of our conversation, he appeared no closer to seeking Jesus. But I wonder. After hearing from Shawn, I'm not so presumptuous.

I wanted to thank Shawn for calling. He left me a phone number, which I dialed repeatedly. Each time I got a recording: "The number you have dialed is temporarily out of service." Just listening to Shawn's message, I suppose, was enough.

Glued to my seat

For a few years, my family dined at the same Italian restaurant one or two Saturdays each month. It became a familiar place with familiar people, from the owner to the wait staff. For two years, nothing unusual happened.

Then one Saturday evening, our routine was disrupted when a car struck a pedestrian in front of us. I didn't see the accident, but I saw the aftermath. I saw the pedestrian grab her leg. I saw the driver pull over to the side of the road. And I heard my wife say we should do something.

I said no. It looked to me as if the situation were well in hand, that the two parties were talking to each other, and that there were eyewitnesses on the scene. The woman who had been hurt walked away, apparently unhurt. I returned to my dinner and thought nothing more of the matter.

Until the next morning. After church, a woman came up to my wife and me—the same woman who was struck by the car the night before. When I saw her Saturday night, I didn't recognize her as belonging to our church. When I saw her Sunday morning, I didn't recognize her as the one who was hit Saturday night. She had to make the connections for me.

She told us the story. After being struck, she was in a state of shock. She didn't get any information from the driver or the names of any eyewitnesses. No one called for the police. Aside from a few bruises, she was unhurt.

Had she not come up to us Sunday morning, I would have forgotten about Saturday night. Had I not been at the scene Saturday night, I wouldn't have met her Sunday morning. And

I wouldn't have had to ask myself this question: why did I remain seated Saturday night?

I had concluded that the matter was well in hand, but it wasn't. I observed enough to see what I wanted to see. I remained seated because I didn't want to get involved. I didn't want to get involved because I wasn't sure how to intervene. I was worried that my ignorance and incompetence would be exposed.

Instead, my passivity was exposed. Today, I'm not so much bothered by my ignorance and incompetence. But I am bothered my passivity. I am bothered that I was more concerned with being exposed than with helping someone in need. I'm disturbed that I was more interested in saving my life than losing my life for the sake of Jesus—for the sake of helping someone (Mark 8:34-35).

I think God was addressing a self-protective passivity that too often leaves me glued to my seat. And I think he used the events of one weekend to help me do just that.

Some months later, my family and I saw a driver hit a parked car. I knew what to do. Well, actually, I didn't know what to do; I didn't know how to help her, but I knew that I had to help her. I assessed the situation as best I could. The two cars were virtually attached, and the driver of the parked car was nowhere in sight. I determined that the woman would do further damage to the parked car if she tried to extricate her car. I advised her to call a tow truck and wait for the police.

As we left the scene, my wife noted, "We did something this time."

Yes, we did.

So much

I'm more sensitive than I'd like to be. I'd much prefer to charge up hills fearlessly. Oh, I'll pick my hills, but I'm often wounded by the bullets of criticism that are fired at me. They pierce that part of me that doubts my value.

When wounded, I'm less inclined to invite feedback that might intensify the pain. But I'll often turn to some old friends to help me process the pain: pen and paper. I write. Whatever I feel, I write.

I view personal doubt about my value as a doorway to a deeper relationship with God. Writing about my wounds helps me walk through the doorway. It unlocks my heart so that I might understand my feelings and present my authentic self to God.

One day, when wounded by some comments that challenged my effectiveness as a pastor, I drew up to a table at a local coffee house, where my old friends, pen and paper, came to my aid. Here's what I wrote:

- "I feel like what I do doesn't matter. Maybe I should quit this."
- "It's the lifelong story line: who I am isn't enough."
- "To be rejected, to be ill thought of, is to feel worthless. And I have felt it, despite various successes, my whole life. And what has God done about it? I guess I feel not very much."

Finally, these words came from my pen: "Far from seeking feedback, I tend to avoid it, because it hurts so much."

I was about to start my next sentence when a woman came up to my table and introduced herself as a member of my church. She shook my hand, looked me in the eye, and said, "I appreciate your ministry so much." Her eyes were full of tenderness, and she emphasized the words "so much." Then, like an angel, she left as quickly as she came.

I looked down at the last sentence I had written. My last words and my visitor's last words were identical. Because of my wounds, I was reticent to invite feedback for fear that it would hurt "so much." My visitor, on the other hand, offered uninvited feedback that featured the words "so much" in an affirming way. She matched my words of pain with words of appreciation.

If I had earlier supposed that God had not done very much about my feelings of worthlessness, I now supposed that he had sent one of his people my way to comfort his wounded servant. God, it seems, was offering some feedback of his own: who I am and what I do have value.

The apostle John in his gospel mentions that Jesus restored Peter as they sat around a "fire of burning coals." Earlier in the gospel, he reported that Peter disowned Jesus while standing next to such a fire (John 18:18, 21:9). The scene of Peter's failure became the scene of his restoration. Jesus went to the place of Peter's brokenness and healed him there. The fire of burning coals meant failure to Peter, but Jesus used it to restore him.

The words "so much" meant failure to me, but Jesus used them to restore me.

I didn't quit.

WHAT HE DIDN'T SEE

In the summer of 2006, I met regularly with a man who felt the time had come for him to investigate the claims of Jesus. Paul had moved to the Silicon Valley more than eight years earlier and was still trying to find his way vocationally. He prepared for our Bible studies by thoroughly examining the passages. I enjoyed his keen mind and open heart. We bonded over an appreciation for literature. But I was not able to lead him to faith in Christ.

One day, I received a letter from him. He thanked me for meeting with him but told me he was leaving the next day to return to the East Coast. In the letter, he shared with me some reflections on the Valley:

What has become of the people in the Bay Area? They seem shallow to the degree that they are affluent. This land, "The Valley of Heart's Delight," is bountiful and beautiful. On my first day (February 20, 1998) out here, I was stunned to see orange trees, their branches bending heavy with fruit. In the depths of winter, trees bore fruit. That same day I noticed something else: sports cars— Porsche Boxsters, Miatas—everywhere. Two seats only, little room for groceries. Of what use were these cars? Now, leaving, I keep remembering Steinbeck's *The Grapes of Wrath*. Some seventy years ago, he wrote it in Monte Sereno, not far from here. The story is timeless. People migrate to California seeking to better their lives by working the abundance here. Pick fruit, write computer code. If you've got energy and enthusiasm, you can make it here. Or so you believed as an article of faith. And the land *is* bountiful, even more than expected, but what becomes of that bounty? What does it do to the people who possess it? And to the people who don't possess it? I've been a stranger in a strange land for these eight and one-half years, living not in my own home or apartment but in a rented room. I was too busy working to exercise stock options or to buy a sports car. I worked like the "Okies" in Steinbeck's novel worked. I'm proud of that, but I also have come to understand: I don't belong here.

Maybe he's right—about the people, or at least many of the people, and about himself. If Paul had become acquainted with some of my friends from church, however, he may have written a different sort of letter. True, many are affluent, but many are not. None would I describe as shallow. They know they're broken and therefore know they need Jesus. They're seeking to follow him in the way of self-giving love. I am sorry that I didn't introduce Paul to them.

I've conducted an informal survey in my travels. When I meet a believer who was not reared in the church and ask what drew him or her to Jesus, the answer usually goes something like this: "There was something about these people who were following Jesus—something about the way they loved each other, something about the way they loved me."

When I read Paul's letter, I immediately remembered similar meetings I had with another man a few years earlier. Joe and I met weekly for two years to investigate the claims of Jesus. At first we met with two men from the church. I took him golfing with other church friends. He began attending one of our classes, where he was exposed to still more believers. He often noted that he was encouraged by the way the church folks related to each other and to him. What he saw in the people of Jesus finally helped convince him of the reality of Jesus. In the end, he committed his life to Christ.

The Scriptures say that exposure to Jesus' worshiping community is so powerful that it can cause an unbeliever to fall down and proclaim, "God is really among you!" (1 Corinthians 14:25).

Joe saw what Paul didn't see. I showed Joe something I didn't show Paul. Paul never saw the people of Jesus loving each other and extending love to him. The best witness for Jesus that I could have given him was the community of Jesus, and I didn't give it to him.

The next time I meet someone like Paul, I think I'll do with him what I did with Joe. I'll introduce him to my church.

WHAT'S IN A NAME? (PART TWO)

After sensing God's direction in the naming of our first child, Christina, I had wondered if he would be similarly involved when it came time to name our second child. The first time, the selection of a name was a months-long process. The second time, my wife Karen and I chose a name the minute we started thinking about one. God, I think, was no less involved.

The biblical story of the raising of Lazarus inspired me when I read it as a teenager shortly after I began following Jesus. Jesus' words concerning Lazarus' illness encouraged me: "This sickness will not end in death. No, it is for God's glory so that God's Son may be glorified through it" (John 11:4). In later years, I was both comforted and challenged by Jesus' words to Lazarus' two sisters, Mary and Martha. I've taught the story in numerous settings as a pastor, including on a sidewalk in Israel next to what is reputed to be the tomb of Lazarus.

Four months before our second child was born, I was invited to preach at a neighboring church, which was in the middle of a year-long study of the gospel of John. After accepting the invitation, I learned that my assignment would be John 11, which features the raising of Lazarus. I came prepared with a teaching outline, but seconds before I got up to preach, these words formed in my mind: "You know this stuff." I wondered if God was nudging me to preach without any notes. So I left my notes on the chair and preached the story with a freedom that connected me to God, the text, and the congregation.

Two weeks later, we went on a family vacation. Based on ultrasound images, we were expecting a girl. As we lay in bed

164

one night, Karen began reading off potential names. One of the first names was Bethany. I thought, "That's it." Karen liked it too.

The village of Bethany was the home of Mary, Martha, and Lazarus. Jesus came to Bethany, first to enlarge the faith of the two sisters and then to raise their brother from the dead.

Unlike the selection of a name for our first daughter, when we settled on names only to dismiss them a few weeks later, we stayed with Bethany and never wavered. We immediately enjoyed the first name we thought of for our second child just as much as we enjoyed the name we eventually chose for our first child.

The same task—naming a child—involved different approaches. God led in both cases, but in different ways.

God leads, but he's unpredictable. He may lead us to approach apparently identical tasks differently. In the gospels, Jesus heals, but in different ways. In the village of Bethany, two sisters were grieving the same loss, but Jesus spoke differently to each.

In the case of our second daughter, God led us to choose a name that he had been weaving into my life since I began following Jesus. Bethany, in a sense, has been with me all these years. Now two sisters, Christina and Bethany, are growing up together, like Mary and Martha. If Jesus comforts and challenges them so that they come to believe that God will be glorified through whatever losses they suffer, their father will be pleased.

THE SECOND DAY

For me, the first afternoon of a two-day personal retreat often unnerves me. I enjoy the drive to the site in the morning, but once I arrive and close the doors to my room, I feel trapped.

On one such afternoon, the walls closed in on me. Here's what I wrote in a journal: "I'm at a loss. Nothing. Blank. I can't wait. I can't just be. Wrestlings and anguish. Restless. No peace. No direction." I wrote in staccato because I couldn't generate the energy for anything more. During the afternoon and evening, I read a few psalms and gave some attention to the Parable of the Prodigal Son in Luke 15. Nothing helped. Finally, I collapsed in exhaustion and fell into a deep sleep at 9:00 p.m.

At my home, I have difficulty falling asleep and staying asleep. If I sleep for six hours, I'm thankful. Seven is heaven, I say. On this retreat, I slept soundly for eight hours, waking up at 6:00 a.m. When I woke, the Parable of the Prodigal Son returned to my mind—or maybe it had been with me in some way all night long, for all I know. In the parable, a father welcomes home his rebellious younger son by killing the fattened calf. The resentful older son complains that his father hasn't given him so much as a goat. Especially, I fixated on the father's words to the older son in Luke 15:31: "Son, you are always with me, and all that is mine is yours." The father in the parable represents the heavenly Father, who welcomes both obvious sinners (the younger son) and not-so-obvious sinners (the older son). The older son wants a goat but doesn't realize that he already has everything.

When I woke, I sensed the Father telling me, "Son, you are always with me, and all that is mine is yours." Really? Everything? I looked out my window, to the Tomales Bay below and to the hills beyond, and beyond the hills to the endless horizon. At sunrise, it dawned on me—as it had never dawned on me before—that God has already given me everything. The Tomales Bay, the hills, the horizon, the heavens and the earth: God created everything for us. Although the heavens and the earth groan because we rebelled against God, God promises to re-create them. I am with the Father. All creation is mine. What more do I want? A goat?

I spent the next four hours reveling in Luke 15:31. I meditated on the Father's love for me. I delighted in what he has given me and what he will give me.

On the first day of the retreat, I was despairing; on the second day, I was rejoicing. On the first day, nothing helped; on the second day, one verse—a verse I had, in fact, read the day before—changed everything. On the first day, the walls closed in on me; on the second day, a window into heaven opened up.

What happened? On the first day, I lamented. When the psalmists lament, they're not complaining; they're seeking a new perspective. When a cup is emptied, it can be filled with something else. On the first day, I emptied my cup of despair; on the second day, God filled it with joy.

Maybe I should get away more often.

Chapter 6

WHAT DREAMS BECOME

Something better

When I was twenty years old, I began to dream about writing on the coast. A friend and I were driving on Highway 1 near Half Moon Bay, south of San Francisco. It was a stormy winter day. The cypress trees, bending in the wind, looked like they might blow over. She said maybe we'd get married some day and live on the coast. She'd be a lawyer and I'd be a writer. It's the kind of thing you say, I guess, when you're young and a moment overtakes you. We weren't even dating at the time.

She married someone else, of course. I remained single.

Her comment returned to me occasionally, especially when I visited the coast, and it triggered a different dream. I pictured myself alone in the winter. Outside, the wind and rain would be pounding my coast-side shack, just outside Half Moon Bay. Inside, I'd be wresting poetic prose from my battered soul. Your classic tortured artist. It was more of a nightmare than a dream, I suppose, but it was mine. It seemed romantic.

True to the dream, I went on to be a writer, first as a journalist and then as a pastor. But I never holed up in the shack. When some friends purchased a condominium in Capitola, just south of Santa Cruz, they offered to let me use it. I called them and set aside a week to write in their condominium overlooking the Monterey Bay—in winter, of course.

I spent the week writing in a gorgeous condominium in Capitola, not a rundown shack in Half Moon Bay. The gentle breeze barely rustled the leaves. I never saw a rain cloud. The temperature was warm enough for sunbathing. I wrote fourteen vignettes for this collection, plus the first few lines of this piece. Not once did I wrest anything from my battered soul, for my soul was at rest. At the end of the week, I returned to the woman who had married me seven years earlier and to our two daughters. I couldn't wait to see them.

It took almost thirty years for my dream to grow up. When it did, it became something different. It became something better.

The apostle Paul dreamed of preaching the gospel of Jesus Christ in Spain. He wrote a letter to some folks in Rome in hopes that they would support him in his mission. As far as we know, he never made it to Spain. But his letter made it there. His letter, which became the book of Romans in the Bible, has made it all over the world. It may be the most influential letter ever written. Because Paul dreamed about Spain, he wrote Romans (Romans 15:22-25).

God takes a dream and transforms it into something we could not dream.

HOPE FOR ANOTHER DAY

Danny came into my study and said, "I just had to plop myself down in this chair one more time."

In the ten years that we had served together as pastors, how many times had he done this? In order to enter or exit his study, he had to walk past mine. Danny would often drop by in the course of his comings and goings. Sometimes, a greeting morphed into a conversation. Sometimes, a conversation morphed into what we called "executive session," which featured more sensitive topics. Baseball, theology, church—we discussed pretty much everything. None of these exchanges was ever planned; they just happened as a matter of course. As a matter of course, though, we became good friends. Now he was moving to serve a church in a different part of the country.

My routine always allowed room for Danny's interruptions. In fact, they almost became part of my routine. When I would come home and my wife would ask what I did that day, my answer would sometimes include the words, "I talked with Danny."

His interruptions seemed so normal, in fact, that I didn't realize how important they had become to me. I didn't realize how important Danny had become to me. To have a friend with whom to share the spectrum of life's concerns, and to be able to do so spontaneously, without picking up a phone, without writing an e-mail, without scheduling a meeting—what is that worth?

I had never really considered this until the day Danny dropped by my study for the last time. We chatted for a few minutes—

shared a few memories, peered into the future. I tried to soak it in because I knew that Danny and I would never talk like this again. Oh, we'd trade e-mails and talk on the phone. We'd see each other again, but to do so we'd have to schedule a meeting.

We embraced and said we'd miss each other. Then Danny walked out of my study, just like so many times before. Only this time, I watched him as he left—watched each step until he was through the door, around the corner, and gone.

I wasn't good for much of anything the rest of the day. When my wife asked me about my day, I broke down. I could tell her, as I often told her, that Danny stopped by my study. But I wept because I knew I would never be able to say that again.

My sorrow that day made me hope for another day—a day when there will be no more tears. On that day, Danny and I will serve the Lord together again, along with all those who believe in Jesus Christ. That day will feature God's new creation, and it will never end (Revelation 21:1-22:5).

Wherever I am, Danny can stop by any time he likes.

This I can say

My preferred approach to preaching is to pick a book of the Bible and teach through it, week by week, until I'm finished with it. One book, more than any other, has fascinated me: the apostle Paul's letter to the church in Rome. It is, quite possibly, the most analyzed letter ever written.

Not long after I became a pastor, Romans became for me the *Moby-Dick* of biblical books because of its interpretive puzzles. I began to dream about preaching it. I did not think, however, that I was ready for it. So I began doing some background work. During a sabbatical in 2001, I studied Romans. When my first daughter was born in 2003, I took three weeks off and studied Romans in between diaper changes.

In 2004, another pastor at our church wanted to preach Romans.

"Can't do it," I said.

"Why not?" he said.

"Because I'm going to do it."

I couldn't put it off much longer. I would never be as ready as I wanted to be. I took a year to translate Romans, from Paul's Greek to my English, in order to better understand it. Finally, in January 2006, I preached my first sermon on Romans. In all, I preached twenty-seven sermons in my Romans series, finishing in June 2007.

When I study the text, I try to give it access to my life. Then, if all goes well, the church hears from a pastor who has been shaped by the text he's preaching. I dreamed of preaching Romans, but I didn't know what Romans would do to me.

I didn't know what it would do to our church. One member said it created a renaissance. Another said my sermons weren't challenging enough. So I still don't know what it did to our church. I can't know all that it did to me, either. Who can say all of what the Holy Spirit does with God's word?

This, however, I can say: in studying Paul's letter, I became convinced that he wrote it because he wanted the Roman believers in Christ to live as a community. The church, he says, is the body of Christ, and its members are supernaturally connected to each other (Romans 12:4-5). Studying Romans and preaching it—not to some anonymous assemblage but to my church—made me feel connected to the people to whom I was preaching. I would stand up each week and think, "These are my people." The Spirit used the word to solidify my relationship with the members of the body of Christ.

The one who thinks I created a renaissance . . . I belong to him. The one who thinks my sermons weren't challenging enough . . . I belong to him, too. When I dreamed of preaching Romans, I didn't dream it would teach me these things.

BE STRONG AND WORK

Early on, a ministry to young adults that I had started involved more than a hundred people. Some years later, only about a dozen were involved. With attendance dwindling and no new leaders on the horizon, I considered killing the Young Adults Fellowship. But just as I was about to pull the plug, six new leaders emerged.

The new leaders drew close to each other. They sought the Lord for fresh vision. They decided they wanted the fellowship to bless their church and their world. They embraced newcomers, who quickly began speaking of the fellowship as their family. Members of the fellowship sort of invaded the church, serving in a multitude of ministries. Weekly attendance grew to only twenty, but those twenty were everywhere.

I had to admit, though, that when the fellowship involved one hundred, I had felt more effective as a leader. But I couldn't deny that the Spirit of God was present and active in the twenty. Is one hundred better than twenty? Or is twenty just different from one hundred?

After finishing a twelve-week preaching series, I came to our church worship service without any responsibilities. Mo, a woman who had helped lead the Young Adults Fellowship when it involved more than one hundred, was hosting the service. Paul, our newest pastor, was preaching from Haggai 2:1-9, which recounts a prophet's exhortation to the people of Israel to continue rebuilding the temple, which the Babylonians had destroyed.

The people were discouraged because it was already apparent that the new temple would not match the glory of the old temple. Nevertheless, the prophet told them to get to work and that the Lord would help them. The Lord was just as involved with the new temple as he was with the old temple. The new temple wouldn't be as big or beautiful as the old temple, but from the Lord's perspective, it was just as important.

At the conclusion of Paul's sermon, Mo asked the worshipers to reflect on how they saw God working in the present. Immediately, I thought of the Young Adults Fellowship and looked at its members, who were seated nearby. When Mo spoke again, I turned back to her. In two glances, I saw—quite literally—how the text applied to me. I saw members of the new fellowship worshiping near me, and I saw Mo, from the old fellowship, leading me in worship.

The Lord was involved with the old fellowship, just as he was involved with the old temple, and he was involved with the new fellowship, just as he was involved with the new temple. One hundred is different from twenty, I concluded, but twenty can be just as good.

The Lord told the people of Israel, "Be strong and work. For I am with you." I think he was speaking to me also.

LUCKY MAN

I had a difficult time relaxing at restaurants while dining with my two daughters when they were small. Like many children, they were not wired for sitting still in a public place.

While we were on vacation, my wife and I decided to take our girls to a beachfront restaurant. From the moment we sat at our table, I was on the alert, concerned that one of the girls would spill something or break something if I looked away for a moment. What I really wanted to do, as the sun set into the Pacific, was to alternately gaze into the eyes of my wife and out the window for the breathtaking view. I adore my daughters, but there are times when I long for more one-on-one time with my wife. Our trip to the beachfront restaurant was such an occasion.

I was lamenting silently when I heard a voice coming from behind me. I had the sense that someone was speaking to me. As I turned around, I saw a man approaching me from the bar. "What?" I asked him.

"You're a lucky man," he said.

"What?"

"You're a lucky man."

He reached out to shake my hand. The lines on his face told me he was in his forties. His expression told me he was in pain.

What had he seen as he saw me dining with my family? What motivated him to leave the bar and speak to me? What did he see when he shook my hand?

I had what he wanted, I presume: a family. Did he lose his family? Was he suffering from a recent breakup? Was he grieving over a long-ago road not taken? I don't know. As soon as he shook my hand, he turned and walked away, out of the restaurant and into the night.

When I turned back to my family, I did so with a different perspective. I was out on the town with my family: my beautiful wife and my totally alive daughters. Indeed, I was a lucky man.

Naomi, whose name meant "Pleasant," was a lucky woman: she had a husband and two sons. She and her family left their home in Bethlehem for a while to sojourn in a different land. Then, tragedy struck: Naomi's husband died. Her sons married women from that land. Then, tragedy struck again: her two sons also died. When Naomi returned to Bethlehem, Ruth, the widow of one of her sons, came with her. The whole town turned out to greet her, wondering if she was, in fact, Naomi. She replied that Mara, which means "Bitter," would be a more appropriate name for her, noting, "I went away full, but the Lord has brought me back empty."

Empty? Ruth was with her. Naomi didn't know it at the time, but Ruth would marry Boaz and give birth to Obed, who would become the father of Jesse, who would become the father of David (Ruth 1, 4:13-22). Matthew, in the first chapter of his gospel, tells the rest of the story, listing the descendents of David leading up to Jesus, the Messiah.

Naomi didn't know it, but when she came to Bethlehem with Ruth, she was returning with the future of humanity. When Obed, the ancestor of the Messiah was born, Naomi laid him in her lap and cared for him. She was a lucky woman, even when she thought she was empty. Eventually, her perspective changed.

While dining with my family in the beachfront restaurant, my perspective changed.

From time to time, I think about the man who left the bar to shake my hand, especially when I feel challenged by family life. He doesn't know it, but he gave me a gift: the gift of perspective. I hope that his luck has changed—or that someone does for him what he did for me and prompts him to see things differently.

A SERMON OF MANY VOICES

At 8:30 p.m. on a Saturday night, I found out that the pastor who was scheduled to preach at our church the following morning would not be able to make it: the airport he was flying out of was fogged in. As one of our preaching pastors, I spent some time on the phone that night with other leaders trying to determine what to do.

I easily could have filled in by preaching a sermon on short notice. I had preached dozens of sermons that our congregation hadn't heard before; so reworking one of those would not have required much prep time. Nothing would have been wrong with reworking an old sermon—unless, perhaps, God had something else in mind. And that's what I wondered: did God have something else in mind? It seemed to me that we had planned for a sermon but that God, for whatever reason, had thwarted our plans. To replace a sermon with another sermon didn't feel right to me.

As I spoke on the phone with one of the other pastors, 1 Corinthians 14, a chapter I had been pondering for some time, came to mind. When the Corinthian church gathered, everyone participated. The apostle Paul, the author of 1 Corinthians, sought to bring order to the church's chaotic gatherings but nevertheless affirmed its participatory approach: "When you come together, everyone has a hymn, or a word of instruction, a revelation, a tongue or an interpretation. All of these must be done for the strengthening of the church" (1 Corinthians 14:26). When 1 Corinthians 14 came to mind, I knew what I wanted to do. I wanted to infuse our worship services the next day with the ethos of that chapter.

On Sunday, I stood before our worshipers, read from 1 Corinthians 14, and invited them to share their joys and sorrows, their praises and laments, their insights and reflections. "Today, you're the sermon," I told them.

They responded eagerly and shared openly. If they were the sermon, they preached beautifully. Several of the worshipers were so taken by what transpired in the first service that they stayed for the second service. So many people shared during the second service that it went well past the time we normally end.

Finally, I was about to close the second service when a woman stepped forward and shyly volunteered to perform a song that she had just written during a particularly dark period in her life. Then she sat down at the piano and sang—haltingly at times, but with piercing honesty. After that, I closed the service, even if I could barely get the words out, so moved was I by what we had experienced as a church.

Our leadership team surmised that God, by thwarting our plans and blessing us with an extraordinarily rich Sunday, was telling us something. From then on, we decided to set aside fifteen minutes in our worship services every month for congregational sharing.

The church, Paul says, is the body of Christ. Each part of the body has contribution to make; each person *is* a contribution. I take it that when God thwarted our plans and gave us a sermon of many voices, he did so "for the strengthening of the church."

THE SONG OF A NEW WORLD

We were exposed to some heart-wrenching stories during a missions trip to India: extreme poverty, dozens of HIV cases, and abusive family relationships among them. Most of the people we treated at our free medical clinics were Dalits, "untouchables" who occupied the lowest rung in society.

During meals and debriefing sessions at the end of each day, some members of our medical team broke down in tears because of what they were encountering. They were groaning for the patients they were treating and for their inability to help in any substantive way. To some extent, I groaned also, but to a greater extent, I groaned for the groaners: I was affected by how the team members were affected.

One Sunday while we were in India, I was asked to preach at a local church. How does a preacher decide what to preach? Sometimes, I agonize over such decisions. This time, the decision was easy. As I heard the groans of the medical team, I remembered the groans that the apostle Paul writes about in Romans 8:18-30.

Creation groans, Paul says. "Not only so, but we ourselves, who have the firstfruits of the Spirit, groan inwardly as we wait eagerly for our adoption as sons, the redemption of our bodies"(Romans 8:23). Finally, the Holy Spirit groans. What's all this groaning about? It's about the longing for a new world: a world without poverty, HIV, and abusive family relationships, a world in which no one is untouchable.

Paul says that God will take the groaning of creation, the groaning of his people, and the groaning of his Spirit and give birth to a new creation. Together, at the direction of the great Maestro, the groans harmonize to sing the song of the new world. If you listen carefully to Romans 8, you can hear that song. And if you can hear it, you can tune your life to it.

Inspired by the groans of the medical team, I decided to preach on Romans 8:18-30. About a dozen of our team members joined me for the worship service. When the worship service began, there were only a handful of local church members in attendance. Then, this thought occurred to me: this sermon might be for our people as much as it is for the Indians. After all, my experience of our people persuaded me to preach on Romans 8 in the first place. Sure enough, as I stepped up to preach, the members of our church outnumbered the members of the Indian church two-to-one.

As I preached, I felt connected to the Indian worshipers, to be sure, but even more so to the members of the medical team. I wanted to validate what they were feeling and assure them that their groans were not in vain.

I'm not sure that I've ever preached to a smaller congregation. But I'm also not sure I've ever preached with more compassion. After the worship service, many members of our team told me that the sermon encouraged them greatly. In fact, almost a year later, I ran into a team member at a restaurant who told me that the sermon was one of the highlights of her trip.

When I signed up for the India trip, I never would have guessed that I was also signing up to travel halfway around the world to preach to my own church.

MEMORY OF A MAN

At the conclusion of a weeklong pastors' conference in Bangalore, India, my two colleagues and I were receiving the seventy attendees, many of whom expressed appreciation for our exposition of the biblical texts at the conference. One of the pastors, a young man, probably in his twenties, approached me with a desperate look on his face and a tremor of urgency in his voice.

Fighting back tears, he said, "You should stay in India," and I had no doubt that he was serious. Clearly, our teaching from the Scriptures satisfied some desire within him and made him long for more. The word of God is like that for some people: it nourishes them while at the same time increasing their hunger. I politely indicated that I could not remain in India because my home was in the United States.

I returned to California, but the memory of my encounter with the pastor in India haunted me like a recurring dream. In my mind, I kept seeing his face and hearing his words.

In a vision, the apostle Paul saw a man and heard him say, "Come over to Macedonia and help us." Based on the vision, Paul and his companions concluded that God had called them to travel to Macedonia and preach the gospel there. So they departed from Troas and traveled to the Macedonian city of Philippi, where they planted a church (Acts 16:9-12). Later, after he departed, Paul wrote a letter to the church in Philippi that became part of the New Testament.

I received no vision; I saw a real man who spoke real words. But when the memory of my encounter with him remained with me, it became to me something like a vision. One day, when the memory reappeared, I remembered Paul's vision. Like Paul, I concluded that God was calling me to go somewhere—in my case, to India again. When the man had asked me to stay in India, I didn't stay, but India stayed with me—so much so that I had to go back. So the following year, I returned to Bangalore to teach at another pastors' conference, bringing with me three new teachers.

At the conclusion of the first trip, during the closing ceremonies for the pastors' conference, I choked up when commending the Indians for their passion. "We have more knowledge, which I think is why God lets us get up here and teach you," I told them, my voice cracking. "But you have more passion." At the conclusion of the second trip, I choked up again, but not when commending the pastors for their passion, though commend them I did. Instead, my voice cracked when I commended the three teachers whom I brought with me—two men and one woman who had been trained by our church. The three of them had served so well, teaching and loving the Indians throughout the conference, and all of them preached at churches in India on the Sunday following the conference. They showed me the value of our investment in them—and the value of continuing to make such investments.

Now I see that I needed to return to India—for the Indian pastors, for the three teachers I took with me, and for me. God calls, through visions or memories or the Scriptures, or through any combination thereof, or through any of a thousand other ways, I suppose, to get his people to the right place at the right time for his purposes.

THE FIRST PSALMS

How can the Scriptures on the one hand contend that "God is love" while on the other hand report that he ordered the eradication of entire nations? Theologians have their answers. I, too, have my ready-made answers, many of which have been generated from my reading of the theologians. Not until I visited a slum in India, however, did I get a feel for how God's anger and love can justly coexist.

Our church has partnered with a missionary organization to bring medical teams to India. When the organization seeks to bring the gospel to a slum in India, it sets up a medical clinic in that slum. Normally, after people go through the clinic, they are funneled to men and women who will pray for them. However, when introducing the gospel to a slum, the organizers seek to earn trust. They want to heal for the sake of Jesus before they mention the name of Jesus. Therefore, for first-time medical clinics, organizers send patients on their way after they've been treated instead of publicly praying for them.

When our church sends a medical team to India, we send not only doctors, nurses, and pharmacists but also pray-ers. I have served in the prayer ministry. But when the leaders of the missionary organization sent us to a new slum, they asked us, according to their custom, not to engage in a public prayer ministry. I accompanied the medical team to the slum but, without any medical skills to speak of, wondered what I would be doing.

As our medical team began seeing patients, those whom Mother Teresa called the poorest of the poor, I had an idea. I called the other members of the prayer team together and said, "Let's read the Psalms." So the four of us gathered in a cordoned-off area inside the large tent and began reading the Psalms aloud, but softly, to each other, starting with Psalm 1.

The first compositions in the Psalter contain many references to the anger of God:

- "Then he rebukes them in his anger / and terrifies them in his wrath . . ." (Psalm 2:5).
- "God is a righteous judge, / a God who expresses his wrath every day" (Psalm 7:11).
- "The earth trembled and quaked, / and the foundations of the mountains shook; / they trembled because he was angry. / Smoke rose from his nostrils; consuming fire came down from his mouth, / burning coals blazed out of it" (Psalm 18:7-8).

As the four of us read the Psalms, I glanced up occasionally to see the empty faces of the slum dwellers who had crowded into the tent to see a doctor. At first, I didn't enjoy reading about the anger of God, but the more I read, and the more I listened to my friends read, the more I resonated with God's anger. I wasn't alone. One of my prayer partners commented, "I feel as if we're reading about what's happening before us." Yes, of course God gets angry! *I* was angry—angry because of such dehumanizing poverty and despair, and I wanted God to be angry, too. The Psalms confirmed for me that he *was* angry: mountain-shaking, nostril-flaring, fire-breathing angry.

In a slum in India, God opened for me a small window into the unification of his anger and his love: God is angry because of dehumanizing poverty and despair, but in his love, he sent a collection of his people to do something about it. Yes, it was a very small something, but it was also the beginning of something, for the organization we partnered with planned to set up another medical clinic in the slum, and then another, with the hopes of one day planting a church, where people could be renewed, and a school, where children could get an education, and yet more medical clinics, where they could feel the healing touch of Jesus. Perhaps Jesus' Parable of the Mustard Seed will come true in that slum, for the mustard seed, though it is small, grows to be large, "with such big branches that the birds of the air can perch in its shade" (Mark 4:30-32). One day, the Scriptures say, the wrath of God and the love of God will be completely satisfied, and earth and heaven will be one. For in the first Psalms, there is also this:

"The needy will not always be forgotten, / nor the hope of the afflicted ever perish" (Psalm 9:18).

And this:

"'Because of the oppression of the weak / and the groaning of the needy, / I will now arise,' says the Lord. / 'I will protect them from those who malign them'" (Psalm 12:5).

And this:

"You hear, O Lord, the desire of the afflicted; / you encourage them, and you listen to their cry, / defending the fatherless and the oppressed, / in order that man, who is of the earth, may terrify no more" (Psalm 10:17-18).

THE FIRST GAME

I was seven years old, I think, when my grandfather and my uncle took me to my first Major League Baseball game. We ascended the steps of Candlestick Park in San Francisco and sat in the top row, up with the seagulls and the clouds, which I assumed was the best place to watch a ballgame because you could both spread out (no one else was seated near us) and see all the action without turning your head.

The Giants defeated the Dodgers that day, throwing out Maury Wills, the game's best base stealer, and knocking Sandy Koufax, the game's best pitcher, out of the box.

"Where's he going, Grandpa?" I asked as Koufax exited the field.

"He's going to the showers."

"To the showers?"

I didn't understand why a player had to leave the game or visit "the showers" afterward. What I didn't understand, though, didn't prevent me from enjoying the game. (I later came to understand that the expression means removal from the game— i.e., the player, finished for the day, takes a shower in the locker room.) In fact, I was enthralled. When the Giants recorded the final out in the top of the ninth inning, all the players left the field: the game was over. I did not yet know that the home team doesn't bat in the bottom of the ninth if it is leading after the visiting team bats in the top of the inning. I deemed this rule unfair. I thought that if the Dodgers batted in their half of the inning, then the Giants should get to bat in their half, even if victory had already been assured. My real problem, though, was that I wanted to watch more baseball. I didn't want the game to end.

Thus began a lifelong love affair with the game. I played baseball in youth leagues and in high school; as a fan, I have attended my share of games through the years. I always hoped that if I had children, they would want to attend baseball games with me. So, when my oldest daughter turned seven, I took her to her first baseball game, a minor league contest in San Jose.

I was worried that Christina would be bored and that she'd be begging to leave before the game was half over. In fact, she was enthralled, though she didn't understand everything. She was especially taken by the off-beat entertainment between innings. I was caught up in her wonder, standing and cheering with her so much that the teenagers behind me finally shouted, "Down in front!"

The game lasted longer than expected. By the seventh inning, it was past Christina's bed time, and I suggested to her that we leave. She said she wanted to stay. Finally, after the eighth inning, I insisted that we leave. She begged me to stay, pleading, "I never want it to end!"

Then I remembered: I didn't want the first game I attended to end, either. So we stayed. We stayed for all nine innings, including the bottom of the ninth, which was necessary because the home team, the San Jose Giants, was trailing after the top of the ninth. Half the fans left before the end of the game, but Christina and I stayed for every pitch.

My grandfather had long since died, but my eighty-five-year-old uncle, who I hadn't seen in years, was still alive. The next day, I wrote him a letter, reminding him of my first game and telling him about Christina's first game. Of my first game, I wrote, "I'll never forget it." Of my uncle, I wrote, "I'll never forget you."

Jesus tells us that the Father gives good gifts (Matthew 7:11). Is it too much to suppose that he might even give us love for something as seemingly trivial as a game—a love that unites a father with his daughter, a love that reunites a nephew with his uncle? On a summer night in San Jose, I didn't think so.

Letting go

The creation of a sermon is a work of art. That is to say, it is the work of the Holy Spirit, the divine artist.

Usually, when preparing for a sermon, I start with the biblical text, not a preconceived notion of what I want to say. Even so, when I begin studying, I sometimes have an idea of where the text will take me. I'm almost always wrong. As the sermon takes shape, I have to discard my vision of what I was going to say.

For an Easter sermon, I chose to preach on John 11, the raising of Lazarus. Almost immediately, I envisioned my introduction. I would tell the story of how, twenty-nine years earlier, I had attended the Easter service at the church at which I was now preaching. Back then, I had just lost a cherished relationship, and my career as a journalist was foundering. I came to the church because I knew I needed Jesus. At the time, I had no idea that I would become a pastor one day, much less a pastor of the church I was attending. In the introduction to my sermon, I would even point to exactly where I sat. Good story to begin an Easter sermon with, right? As the sermon took shape, though, my story wouldn't fit, no matter how hard I massaged it. Reluctantly, I let it go.

Finally, as I felt the sermon coming together, I gathered with a few others to plan our worship service. I gave those in attendance an outline of my plans for the sermon, and one of them said I needed some sort of story near the end. I walked away muttering to myself, "Doggone it, I think he's right."

So, back to work—again. I read through the sermon, and when I got to the place where I needed a story, I remembered the illustration that I was going to use for my introduction.

Immediately, it felt right. The more I considered it, the more I realized that it perfectly illustrated the two points I was emphasizing at that place in the sermon: if you believe in Jesus, you may (1) taste the living water and (2) behold the glory of God (John 7:37-38, 11:40). Although I was despondent when I had attended the Easter service twenty-nine years earlier, I nevertheless began sensing the presence of the Lord in new ways during that season of my life. I began drinking more deeply from the living water, and the crystal-clear love of Jesus refreshed me. I began seeing the glory of God, his power and goodness, more profoundly, more frequently, and in more places. When I preached the sermon, I told the story, and I pointed to where I had sat.

The next day, I was told that a member of our church had invited her brother, a skeptic, to attend the Easter service. He came, and he ended up sitting where I had sat twenty-nine years earlier. What's more, he had just lost a cherished relationship. He so identified with my story and was so moved by the worship service that he almost stepped forward to be baptized right then and there. After the service, he told his sister, "I'm close."

The story I had discarded returned to me and landed in the heart of a man in need. That's the work of the Holy Spirit. That's art.

A WALK TURNS INTO A RIDE

I had a half hour to kill after dropping my daughter off for her piano lesson, so I set off by foot to go for a walk in a nearby park. Just then, a woman, also on foot, approached me from the opposite direction with a frantic look on her face and asked me, "Could you tell me where Cupertino is?"

Well, Cupertino is the next town over, I told her, and I pointed in the appropriate direction. Then she wanted to know where to catch the bus that would take her to a job interview in Cupertino. That I could not tell her, so I asked where in Cupertino she wanted to go.

"Homestead Road," she said.

"My car is right here," I said. "I just dropped my daughter off for her piano lesson, I have a half hour on my hands, and I'd be happy to give you a ride."

No sooner had those words escaped from my mouth than I realized that she probably shouldn't get into a car with a man she doesn't know. She hesitated for a moment and then followed me to my car. I felt like apologizing for even offering her a ride and possibly encouraging her to someday make the mistake of getting in the wrong car, so I told her, "You know, you probably shouldn't be getting in a car with a man you don't know." I think that put her at ease.

She was not only desperate for a ride, she was also desperate for a job. She was unemployed and had flown from Boston to the Silicon Valley for the interview. She had been worried that she would be late for the interview, but now she knew that she would be on time, and she couldn't stop thanking me for the ride.

It seemed to me that our encounter was in some way ordained, and I told her so. "I'm a pastor of a church, so I believe in God," I said. "I just dropped my daughter off, I had some time to kill, and my car was only a few steps away. I think God meant for me to give you a ride today."

She said nothing, but a curious look came over her face. I wondered what she was thinking. We conversed for a few minutes more, but nothing came of the God talk. After we found the address she was looking for, she thanked me again and handed me her card as she left for her interview.

Pranka. That was her name.

The next day, I sent her an e-mail and asked how the interview went. I also included the web address of our church.

Pranka wrote back: "Thank you so much for the ride. The interview was good. I'm waiting to hear back from them. Once I move here, I will come to the church for sure."

Philip, an early follower of Jesus, was heading south, from Jerusalem to Gaza, when the Holy Spirit told him to join an Ethiopian who was sitting in his chariot, reading from the book of Isaiah. Philip did so and told the man that Isaiah was writing about Jesus. The man asked Philip to baptize him right then and there. Philip did so, and the man went on his way rejoicing (Acts 8:26-39).

Shortly after my encounter with Pranka, I recalled the story of Philip and the Ethiopian. No, I didn't hear the Spirit tell me to offer her a ride, but something rose from within me, almost against my better judgment, to offer her a ride nonetheless. Pranka wasn't reading the Scriptures; she was looking for a bus. But I was able, at least, to tell her about God. Because of the

197

nature of our encounter, I felt *compelled* to tell her about God. Yes, I now wonder whether the Spirit, in so many ways, told me to offer Pranka a ride.

The book of Acts tells us that the Spirit snatched Philip away after he baptized the Ethiopian and that they saw each other no more. I wonder, though: might I see Pranka again?

A HELPING HAND

It had been some thirty-eight years since I had been on ice skates when my two daughters began pressing me to join them on the ice at a local rink.

As a teenager, I had skated two or three times, with unfortunate results. My ankles continually buckled, so I was never able to achieve anything approaching stability on the ice. I mostly hugged the rail, venturing out into the mainstream only occasionally. After being defeated by the ice, I concluded that my life would be complete if I never again laced up a pair of skates.

However, back then I failed to take into account the persuasive powers of two yet-to-be-born little girls who would share my flesh and blood and take a liking to the ice. After their mother (not I) signed them up for ice skating lessons, Christina, eight years old, and Bethany, five years old, soon began working on me to lace 'em up again. I resisted the girls for a few months, but finally, I capitulated.

I hoped that rental skates had improved since my last foray onto the ice. I painstakingly laced up the boots, making sure they were tight against my ankles. I gingerly placed one skate on the ice, then the other. Indeed, the skates had improved—but I hadn't. My first lap had a painfully familiar feel to it. My ankles buckled as I hugged the rail and tentatively, uh, skated around the rink while my daughters, quite literally, skated circles around me.

What were the girls thinking as they watched their old man wobbling in his long-delayed rematch with the ice? They wanted to help. Christina, the eight-year-old, skated up to tell me,

"Dad, if you move more toward the middle, it's less embarrassing." Yes, she was trying to help. Bethany, the five-year-old, followed by telling me, "Daddy, hold my hand. I'll skate; you glide."

Now, hold on a minute! Up to that point, I had always held her hand to help her. Now, she wanted to hold my hand to help me. So, what could I do as my daughter reached out her hand but reach back? She took off, and we skated around the rink together. Correction: she skated; I glided.

I'm not sure which is more "embarrassing"—hugging the rail or being towed around the rink by a kindergartner. Yet, I felt no embarrassment as Bethany pulled me along, not even a tinge. On the contrary, I felt something like . . . exhilaration.

Jesus reaches out his hand to us, so to speak, and says, "Follow me" (John 1:43). It's a preposterous invitation in this day and age, when what you can see with your eyes and hear with your ears is the measure of all things. Can we reach out to him, even though we can't see him or hear him?

To take a five-year-old by the hand and follow her—preposterous, humbling, yet somehow irresistible, somehow exhilarating. To take Jesus, whom we can't see, by the hand, and follow him—preposterous, humbling, yet maybe irresistible, maybe exhilarating.

He skates; we glide.

CHARLIE

When my high school basketball coach died at the age of eighty-eight, I wept long and hard. Although Charlie Cooke held a special place in my heart, my response to his passing caught me by surprise. It wasn't as if his death wasn't expected; he had been in declining health for years. Why, I wondered, was I so moved?

By the time I played for Charlie, he had already been coaching high school basketball for thirty years. Charlie was a throwback, sporting a crew cut in the seventies when everyone else was growing their hair out. Strong and silent, he deflected all attention away from himself. Charlie did his job without complaining, and he never talked about his emotions. Indeed, I never got the impression that his feelings mattered to him at all. Charlie had a wry sense of humor, which was on display whenever he trotted out stories and anecdotes from his years of coaching.

When I played for him, I think he was having trouble relating to a new generation of teenagers who questioned authority and took drugs. But I was kind of a throwback myself; I never even considered taking drugs, and I figured Charlie knew more about basketball than I did, so I did what he told me. I think I was his kind of guy, though he never told me so outright. I wasn't his most talented player, but he put me in the starting lineup for every game I ever played for him.

As a sort of memorial to Charlie, I dedicated about two hours to remembering everything I could about him.

Before my junior year, there was a sort of coup staged by the junior varsity coach, and Charlie agreed to step down and coach the junior varsity. He never complained. Because

I wasn't good enough to play on the varsity, I played on the junior varsity for Charlie. For my senior year, I moved up to the varsity, but just before the season started, the coach who had staged the coup the previous year had some sort of breakdown and walked away from the team, leaving Charlie to coach both the varsity and the junior varsity. True to form, he never complained.

Early that season, I sprained my ankle during one game, and Charlie dutifully taped it up before every practice and every game for the rest of the year. During another game, I sprained the ankle again, and because it was already tender, the pain was excruciating. As I writhed on the floor, I looked up, and there was Charlie, hovering over me. After the game, one of my teammates told me, "Scott, you should have seen it. As soon as you hit the floor, Mr. Cooke bolted from the bench to be with you. It was as if his own son had fallen."

We didn't have a good team. I think that if Charlie had been able to coach just the varsity instead of two teams, we might have won half of our games. As it was, we lost most of them.

Toward the end of the season, we squared off against our much taller and much better cross-town rival, the eventual league champion. Because our missed shots would almost certainly be rebounded by the other team, Charlie implemented a special ball-control strategy for the game, instructing us to shoot only if we were all but certain that we would score. Alas, we fell behind as usual.

In the second half, however, Charlie's strategy began to work, and we crept back into the game. Converting on the short-range shots, we grew more confident until we took a few ten-footers and even made those. Finally, as we closed the gap, I was open for a sixteen-footer. Although I wasn't sure I had Charlie's approval to take such a shot, I let it fly anyway . . . and it went in.

Remember, I'm the throwback; I do what I'm told, and I wasn't sure whether I had just disobeyed orders. So as I ran to the other end of the court, I passed the bench and sheepishly asked, "Mr. Cooke, am I supposed to take that shot?" By the time I turned around to position myself to play defense, Charlie was up off the bench, grinning and yelling, "Hell yes, shoot it! Shoot it!" I took it that he was telling me, in a sly sort of way, well, as long as you're going to make it, go ahead and shoot it. In the heat of battle, in the biggest game of the year, Charlie could enjoy a special moment with one of his players.

In the final seconds, we pulled off the upset victory, and in the jubilant locker room after the game, Charlie became as emotional as I'd ever seen him. He yelled, "Boys, I told you we were going to knock someone off this year, and we did it!" With that eruption, I think Charlie let off the pent-up frustration of the previous two years—the frustration that he never let anyone see.

Now, after digging up my memories of him, I think I understand why Charlie's passing moved me so. I somehow sensed that Charlie believed in me, even enjoyed me, and I knew that he went the extra mile not only for me but also for all his players. As an insecure teenager, I was casting about for a man who believed in me, who enjoyed me, who thought I was worth his time. I found that man in Charlie.

Since his passing, I've been more intentional about coming alongside men younger than I, and I've renewed myself with the words of the apostle Paul, who came alongside a younger man, Timothy, and instructed him, "And the things you have heard me say in the presence of many witnesses entrust to reliable men who will also be qualified to teach others" (2 Timothy 2:2).

THE BURDEN OF GREATNESS

The leaders of a spiritual retreat I attended encouraged us to reflect on a recent experience and hold it up to the light of Psalm 139.

Immediately, an experience from the previous day came to mind. I had attended a memorial service for a beloved mentor, during which I reunited with a few friends from high school. We sat together and listened to our former youth pastor, Conrad, eulogize "Mr. B," as we called him, and I felt as if I were being transported back in time. There we were, in the same church where we first met almost forty years ago, hanging on Conrad's every word, just like we did back then. After the reception, we poked around the church together, revisiting old haunts and waking up a few echoes.

Back then, as I was coming of age, I found Jesus—and intimacy with his people—and I was revolutionized. Those were days of grace.

With the memorial service in mind, I came to Psalm 139. We were encouraged to read it repeatedly, but I only needed to read it once. These words caught my attention: "All the days ordained for me / were written in your book / before one of them came to be" (Psalm 139:16). I had an issue with this verse. My first thought was, "No they're not. All the days aren't ordained, just some of the days, especially certain days gone by."

I realized that I believed that the days when I was coming of age were graced, and many other days also. But all the days? What about the present days? For me, sometimes, the present doesn't compare to the past, especially when I neglect to be attentive to God in the moment.

After considering Psalm 139, I read the reflections of one of the leaders of the spiritual retreat: "God made you good." Again, I had an issue. The leader was trying to be encouraging, but at that moment, I didn't find his words to be thus. In my case, I think God had a different purpose for those words. "Yes, God made me good," I thought. "But he didn't make me great."

By the next day, I was able to combine the memorial service, Psalm 139, and the leader's reflections into this sentence: "If God had made me great, not just good, the present would be just as glorious as the past." With greater gifts as a leader and a preacher, for example, might I be able to usher in some new age of glory, at least for me and a few others? In prayer, I brought my sentence to God. "Okay, Lord, here's what I'm thinking. What do you think?"

At the end of the retreat, before we came to the Lord's Table, the leaders afforded us the opportunity to pick up a flower or a stone and set it next to the bread and the cup—a flower for a joy or a stone for a burden. I picked up a stone, and it felt like greatness. As I came forward to partake of the meal, I released the stone.

What does God think? I think he wants me to lay down the burden of greatness and let him be great.

And, of course, there's this from Jesus: "You know that those who are regarded as rulers of the Gentiles lord it over them, and their high officials exercise authority over them. Not so with you. Instead, whoever wants to become great among you must be your servant, and whoever wants to be first must be slave of all" (Mark 10:42-44).

THE UNNECESSARY DUFFEL

Before a camping trip, I made a list of items to pack and filled my duffel bag with everything I expected to need for a six-day camping trip with about a hundred other people from our church. Most people make such lists. What most people don't do is include in their lists a note that says something like, "Put duffel bag in car." I didn't write myself such a note, either.

You wouldn't think such a note would be necessary, but as we pulled into the campsite, some two hundred and fifty miles from home, I suddenly couldn't recall putting my duffel bag in the car before we had left.

Sure enough, when we emptied the trunk and transported items to the campsite, my duffel bag was not among them. I dreaded the prospect of camping for six days in mounds of red dust with neither a change of clothes nor all manner of other necessities. My duffel bag was packed pretty full. My duffel bag was also a six-hour drive away.

What now?

My mood lifted as I saw the humor in it. It made for a good story to share with the other campers, who enjoyed a good chuckle along with me. One of them lent me a shirt, and another even shared a pair of underwear with me.

I also began to wonder whether the hand of God was involved in some way. What are the chances that I would remember to pack everything I needed but forget to pack the duffel bag that contained everything I needed? I've taken hundreds of trips before and never forgotten my baggage. The airlines have failed to deliver my baggage, but I've never forgotten to give it to the airlines.

Trusting that God was involved, I relaxed. Mostly, I forgot about everything I had forgotten. And I had a great time. I learned that I didn't need what I thought I needed.

The apostle Paul learned something similar long before me: ". . . I have learned to be content whatever the circumstances. I know what it is to be in need, and I know what it is to have plenty. I have learned the secret of being content in any and every situation, whether well fed or hungry, whether living in plenty or in want" (Philippians 4:11-12).

What's the secret? This: "I can do all things through him [Christ] who strengthens me" (Philippians 4:13). Knowing Christ gives us strength to be content. Even though I have known the secret for many years, it seems that I still must learn it. Literally, Paul says that he has learned "in the circumstances" to be content. Yes, he has learned to be content whatever the circumstances, but he learned to be content by being in the circumstances. Every situation, therefore, is an opportunity to learn to be content in Christ in that situation.

What did I learn from six days of being "in need"? I learned that I don't need what I think I need, not just on a camping trip but also at home. In the aftermath of my six days in the dust, I began considering which of my possessions I could part with. I need Christ, plus a few other things: "But if we have food and clothing, we will be content with that" (1 Timothy 6:8).

When I returned home, my duffel bag was right where I left it: in my room, beside my bed. I guess I didn't need it.

PRAYER AND PERSPECTIVE

"Psalm 90 was her favorite psalm," he told me. "She had made notes all over it in her Bible."

I therefore made plans to use Psalm 90 as the centerpiece for Janet's memorial service. But the more I read it, the more I questioned whether it would be appropriate for a memorial service. I didn't think, for example, that verse 7, where the psalmist speaks to God, would play very well: "We are consumed by your anger / and terrified by your indignation."

There is much to be said for the wrath of God. We could ask, for example, where would we be without it? If God didn't get angry because of what we do to each other and his creation, I'm not sure what kind of hope we could cling to that he would ever make things better. But there probably isn't much to be said for invoking the wrath of God at a memorial service. Whatever would be said would require a lengthy explanation. I shared these concerns with Janet's family, and they chose other biblical texts to feature at the service. However, although I left Psalm 90 behind, it didn't leave me behind. It stayed with me.

In verse 14, the psalmist prays, "Satisfy us in the morning with your unfailing love, that we may sing for joy and be glad all our days."

The verse articulated what I have come to want most from God. Like everyone else, I want to be satisfied. But what can satisfy me? The psalmist seems to believe that God can satisfy him with his unfailing love. Like the psalmist, I had prayed to experience the love of God, but I'm not sure that I had ever used the psalmist's words. Finding such a prayer in the Scriptures validated my quest and gave me new words, biblical words, to pray. You can't go wrong with a prayer that comes directly from the Scriptures.

Since my encounter with Psalm 90, verse 14 has made a home in my prayer life. Most days, especially in the morning, I pray that the Lord would satisfy me with his unfailing love.

If verse 14 gave me a prayer, verse 1 gave me perspective: "Lord, you have been our dwelling place throughout all generations."

I remember walking alone years ago in the back country of Yellowstone National Park and being struck—why then, I do not know—by the thought that no one knew where I was. As I walked on, I remembered many chapters of my life and many of the people who had played parts in them. No one appeared in every chapter—except for the Lord. I was heartened that, though people I love had come and gone, the Lord had always been with me. He's with me still. Indeed, as Psalm 90 reminds me, the Lord has been my dwelling place for all my years.

I mined Psalm 90 for the sake of Janet's memorial service; instead, Psalm 90, and Janet, who cherished it, gave me a prayer, and it gave me perspective. Satisfy me, Lord, with your unfailing love. The Lord has been my dwelling place throughout all my years.

With a prayer and with perspective: perhaps this is a good way to make an end. Yes, I think I will stop—for now . . . except to tell one more story.

Postscript

ONE MORE STORY

As early as first grade, I enjoyed writing. I've been writing ever since. As a teenager, I wrote for the school paper. In college, I majored in journalism, mostly because it involved writing. After graduating from college, I spent eleven years as a newspaper reporter and editor. Now, as a pastor, I write sermons. Putting words on a page, telling a story, chronicling life—these have been part of me for almost as long as I can remember. Writing has been central to my vocation, both as a journalist and a pastor.

Several years ago, I began wondering if I should expand my writing efforts. I proceeded to bring this question to God countless times. His answer, near as I could tell, was, "Yes. I've given you this gift, and I want you to expand your expression of it." Both friends and strangers have offered unsolicited encouragement to write.

Nevertheless, I had questions. What do I write about? I wanted to write about the spiritual life, but the spiritual life is an enormous topic. Where do I start? With two small children and a full work schedule, where do I find the time? These questions were so daunting that I tried to suppress the desire to write. But I felt like the prophet Jeremiah, who tried to suppress the desire to preach: "But if I say, 'I will not mention him or speak any more in his name,' his word is in my heart like a fire, a fire shut up in my bones. I am weary of holding it in; indeed, I cannot" (Jeremiah 20:9).

I prayed, "If you want me to write, show me what to write, create the time and space, and open doors that I can't open."

Then, I received an e-mail from a woman I hadn't seen in three years. She had attended our church but was critical of both it and me. She now wanted to apologize and ask for my forgiveness. A week later, she arrived in my study for our appointment. She apologized, and I forgave her. Then, unbidden, she launched into another subject:

"Scott, you're a writer. You're a poetic writer. You're able to take the deep things of God and make them understandable to people. You don't know where to start, but that's all right. Just start. Just start writing. You want to write, but you can't find the time to write. A door will open."

I sensed, as soon as she began to speak, that I should listen, especially because I had been praying for help. She didn't know me well enough to speak so perceptively of me. She didn't know about my passion to write or about my prayers. She spoke as if she were looking into my heart. She said she had arrived for our appointment with no intention of speaking to me about writing.

Two months later, a man I had met at a party called me and wanted to have lunch. I thought it would be a friendly get-to-know-you meeting, but he had an agenda.

"I understand that you're a writer," he said. "You need to write."

I told him I planned to wait until my schedule opened up.

"You can't do that!" he said.

I had prayed for God's help, and it seems he answered first by sending a former antagonist and turning her into a prophet and second by sending a mere acquaintance who wouldn't take no for an answer.

God interrupted me. He blocked my way. He showed me a pattern: how he had woven writing into my life from an early age. Once, when seeking him for direction, I sensed these words coming from him: "Tell your stories." God hooked me with his artistry—hooked me right in the heart. So I wrote these vignettes.

I turn, at the last, from narrator to preacher.

Make time in your routine for God, and be alert to interruptions, roadblocks, and patterns. An interruption may signal the presence of God. A roadblock may be God's way of leading you elsewhere. A pattern, theme, or trend in your life may show you God's handiwork. God may use any of these to reveal himself to you. Immerse yourself in the Scriptures. The Scriptures will help you learn the ways of God. If you learn his ways, you'll be better able to recognize them in your life. Read the Scriptures, study them, and assimilate them— and watch for how your story converges with the biblical story.

In these ways, cultivate an appreciation for the artistry of God, for he wants not simply to convince you of his existence and tell you what to do but to hook you in the heart.

Notes

1. Beth Nielsen Chapman, "Old Church Hymns and Nursery Rhymes." Recorded by Waylon Jennings on Eagle (Epic Records, 1990).

2. Rich Mullins and Beaker, "Sometimes by Step" (Noblesville, IN: Kid Brothers of St. Frank Publishing, 1992).

3. Michael W. Smith and Wayne Kirkpatrick, "I'll Lead You Home" (O'Ryan Music Inc. (ASCAP), Emily Boothe Inc. / Magic Beans Music (BMI) administered by Reunion Music Publishing, 1995).

4. David James Duncan, *The River Why* (New York: Bantam Books, 1983), 277-78.

5. *Contact* (Warner Bros., 1997).

6. *A River Runs Through It* (Columbia Pictures, 1992).

7. Irving Stone, *The Agony and the Ecstasy* (New York: Double-day and Co., 1961), 389-91.

8. *Paint Your Wagon* (Paramount Pictures, 1969).

About the Author

Scott C. Grant's experience both as a journalist and a pastor gives him a unique vantage point from which to explore the spiritual life. Whether he's delving into the Scriptures or searching for meaning, he always asks the journalist's question: "What's the story?"

As a pastor at Peninsula Bible Church, he teaches, writes, counsels, and leads the Intern Program, which trains men and women for ministry—and for appreciating the artistry of God in everyday life.

Scott is a sixth-generation San Franciscan who was reared in the Silicon Valley. He is a graduate of both Pepperdine University and the Cole Center for Biblical Studies in Boise, Idaho. His stops as a journalist included stints as a reporter for the *The Record Searchlight* in Redding, California, and as an editor for the *The Contra Costa Times* in Pleasanton, California, where in his off hours he led Bible studies and shepherded high school and college students.

He enjoys looking for God everywhere, especially in the vicinity of trout streams and golf courses. He lives in Sunnyvale, California, with his wife Karen and two daughters, Christina and Bethany.

To read his blog or contact him, go to his web site: www.hookedintheheart.com. To read or listen to his sermons, go to the Peninsula Bible Church web site: www.pbc.org.

www.ingramcontent.com/pod-product-compliance
Lightning Source LLC
La Vergne TN
LVHW051505080426
835509LV00017B/1929